Day by Day with God

Edited by **Jackie Harris** January–April 2025

Writers in this issue

Lyndall Bywater lives in Canterbury and works with The Salvation Army and Canterbury Diocese, helping people pray. She is the author of two books, both published by BRF Ministries: *Faith in the Making* and *Prayer in the Making*.

Liz Hogarth is a freelance writer, subeditor and former Christian journalist who lives in Surrey with her family. She loves to read and jointly runs a book club in her spare time.

Catherine Larner is a freelance writer, editor and presenter who reports on literature, culture and faith for national, regional and Christian magazines and local radio.

The Revd Dr Sara Batts-Neale is a priest in Chelmsford Diocese. She is currently the Anglican chaplain to the University of Essex. Married to Tim, they live with a dog and host a cat.

Tanya Marlow is a lecturer in pastoral theology and a popular speaker and writer. She specialises in *narratio divina* (storytelling in biblical studies) and theologies of disability and suffering. Find her at **TanyaMarlow.com**.

Di Archer is CEO of **tastelifeuk.org**, a charity she cofounded after a family experience of eating disorders. An educator, writer and speaker, she is also resources manager on the CPAS leadership training team.

Jane Walters is chair of the Association of Christian Writers (ACW) and author of *Too Soon* (SPCK). Keen to support emerging writers, she leads an ACW group in her local area of Norfolk as well as creative writing retreats further afield. **janewyattwalters.com** and Instagram: **@readywritersretreats**.

Naomi Aidoo is the founder of Time & Pace® and codirector of Innerscope, an education coaching company she leads with her husband. She is also author of *Finding Flourishing* (BRF, 2024) and contributor to Premier Radio's 'Thought of the Day'. You can find her at **timeandpace.com**.

Elaine Storkey is an academic, author, broadcaster and senior member of Newnham College, Cambridge. A former president of Tearfund, she also directed the London Institute for Contemporary Christianity (LICC) for ten years and has taught in universities both in the UK and overseas.

Finding Flourishing webinar

Date: **Wednesday 19 March 2025**

Time: **8.00 pm (GMT)**

Tickets: **£5.00 or £7.50 to join with a friend**

Book at:
brfonline.org.uk/finding-flourishing-webinar

Join Naomi Aidoo for an hour of teaching and sharing based on her book *Finding Flourishing* in which she explores a Christian view of wellbeing, aiming to point people to Jesus as well as to practical tools to support their flourishing amidst the pressures of life today.

Naomi writes:
> '*Finding Flourishing* is a book in which I share a different perspective on work–life wellbeing: a perspective which doesn't automatically assume you've got everything together and just need a few tweaks, nor place unrealistic expectations on your time. Instead *Finding Flourishing* will enable you to keep going and keep growing in your own time and at your own pace.'

Praise for *Finding Flourishing*:
> 'Written by a busy working mum who knows what she's talking about, *Finding Flourishing* combines practical advice and inspirational content. This book provides a great opportunity to pause, reflect and reorientate our lives around the things that really matter.'
> Ruth Jackson, presenter, Premier Unbelievable

Join this live event, hear Naomi speak out of wisdom and experience, and share your questions and comments.

Welcome

Happy New Year! Thank you for joining us in our Bible studies for 2025. Whether you are entering this new year with energy and excitement or feeling rather drained and anxious, we pray that opening the scriptures each day will encourage you to press on and assure you that Jesus is with you whatever the coming days hold.

As ever, we've chosen a variety of topics to study. Some are topic-based and include references throughout the Bible; others enable us to work through a particular book, narrative or passage.

We begin by delving into the book of Malachi, an Old Testament prophet keen to teach God's people how to practise true religion, but also wanting them to know how just, loving and kind God is. We end by studying God's love in action, as we discover how Jesus fulfilled all Isaiah's visions of the suffering servant, and then we read the resurrection stories that remind us of the wonderful truth that Jesus is with us, always.

In between, we're considering what the Bible says about being creative and the value of silence and solitude, looking in detail at 1 Corinthians 13, exploring what Paul teaches us about the church in his letter to the Ephesians and learning from Saul and Jeremiah.

We also welcome a new writer to the team. Naomi Aidoo is a teacher, author and entrepreneur who is passionate about work–life wellbeing. Naomi writes on how women in the early church contributed to its growth and encourages us to consider our own contribution to building God's kingdom. How might Jesus want to lead us in the months ahead?

A friend recently gave me a pebble inscribed with the beautiful promise from Proverbs 3:5–6: 'Trust in the Lord with all your heart and lean not on your own understanding; in all your ways submit to him, and he will make your paths straight' (NIV). As we begin this new year, may we know that Jesus is with us in every circumstance and situation and remember that he holds the future in his hands. We can trust him to guide us through.

Jackie

Jackie Harris, Editor

Malachi: adjusting our view of God

Lyndall Bywater writes…

Welcome to the book of Malachi, a relatively short prophetic text right at the end of the Old Testament. When you read the contents page in your Bible, it looks a lot like these were the last words recorded in scripture before Jesus came, and though that isn't necessarily the case, we do know that this prophet lived and taught in a time after the people of Israel had returned from exile in Babylon (Persia) and resettled in the land they'd been taken from. The temple had been rebuilt (see the prophecies of Haggai and Zechariah and the story of Ezra), and we're roughly at the point where Nehemiah was about to mastermind the rebuilding of Jerusalem's walls.

Life is relatively stable and prosperous for the people living in the Jerusalem area at this time, and the temple is back up and running, with the Levites re-established as priests and the people familiar again with the rhythms of festivals and sacrifices, worship and prayer.

It's a time of blessing, of challenges having been overcome and nightmares having been parked firmly in the past, yet there's something not quite right. Malachi's messages seem to suggest that the people and the priests have lost sight of the God who did such remarkable wonders for them just a couple of generations ago.

I don't know about you, but I get a bit of a sinking feeling when we delve into an Old Testament prophet's writing. You know it's not likely to be very cheerful, and there's a danger it might not even make much sense to someone living in the 21st century. But bear with me, and with Malachi, as we spend the next week or so hearing these ancient words. There are hard truths to face, but there are gems of grace and hope too. Malachi understands that disillusionment has begun to eat away at his people's faith; they're getting stuck in unwise practices because their view of God has become smaller and smaller. If only they could know how loving, how powerful, how just and how kind God is, then they would find a measure of freedom unlike any even their ancestors had known. Let's go with them in search of that same freedom.

7

First things first

A prophecy: the word of the Lord to Israel through Malachi. 'I have loved you,' says the Lord. (vv. 1–2, NIV)

A very happy New Year to you! I have a little collection of new year's resolutions which I regularly make and then break again, and one of those is the resolution to stop having unhelpful imaginary conversations with people in my head. You know the ones I mean: you feel misunderstood by someone, so you spend the next three days arguing with them in your head, getting more and more het up, and all the while they know nothing about it. Every year I tell myself I'll kick the habit, and every year I keep having those imaginary conversations.

Imagine my surprise then when I began to study the book of Malachi for these Bible notes, only to discover God having an imaginary conversation with the people of Israel. Malachi records six different chunks of this conversation, and we'll be spending the next week and a half listening in.

Although some parts of this conversation make uncomfortable reading, the whole thing begins with an utterly glorious statement. Before God says anything else, God simply says: 'I have loved you.'

That's it, isn't it? We could close this book right now and just take those four words as our watchword for the year. God has loved us. No matter what we've done, God has loved us. Whether we step into this new year with enthusiasm or trepidation, grief or joy (or maybe all four), God has loved us. We may feel we've failed, that we don't deserve God's love, but God has loved us. Even if we've forgotten God altogether, God has loved us.

As you contemplate 2025, hold in your mind this staggering truth, that the God of all creation has loved you from before the dawn of time and will go on loving you no matter what happens this year.

Consider taking these four words, 'I have loved you', as your watchword for this year. Savour them in your mind as you might savour a sweet in your mouth. Read Jeremiah 31:3–7 for another declaration of this beautiful truth.

LYNDALL BYWATER

Let's get recentred

'You will see it with your own eyes and say, "Great is the Lord – even beyond the borders of Israel."' (v. 5, NIV)

I'm blind, and though it may sound obvious, one of the most frustrating things about my disability is not being able to see what's happening around me. That's particularly tricky when someone is helping me, and in their zeal to make sure all my needs are met, they put other people in a difficult or uncomfortable position. Imagine my embarrassment when I realise that, in a bid to find me a seat on a train, the assistance person has turned a parent with a small child out of a seat they badly needed. I'm grateful for the help, but I wish I'd known what was going on so I could make a choice that would help everyone around me, not just me.

Today's passage continues Malachi's report of the conversation God is imagining with the people of Israel. Having given that beautiful reassurance of eternal love, God knows exactly what's coming next, the oft-repeated cry: 'It's not fair; everyone else has it way better than us.' I confess to feeling uncomfortable when I read verses which talk of God hating certain tribes or nations, even if they are deemed to be evil, but what I see here is God inviting the people to look up from their own pain to see a bigger picture. They may feel hard done by, but when they look at their fortunes in comparison to the fortunes of their near neighbours, they have much to be thankful for.

It's a profound privilege to be able to get perspective – to look up and see our own lives within the bigger picture of what's happening around us. What's more, it's a profound privilege to be able to choose to be thankful for what we have and to put our own needs and frustrations aside in order to bless others.

Is there a situation which has been consuming your focus lately – maybe even making you feel hard done by? Ask God to help you look up from it today, and spend some time praying for someone else who's facing tough times.

LYNDALL BYWATER

Bringing the best

'Why doesn't one of you just shut the Temple doors and lock them? Then none of you can get in and play at religion with this silly, empty-headed worship.' (v. 10, MSG)

Presents can be a complicated thing, can't they? I trust you got some lovely gifts for Christmas, but I'm guessing you might have got a few which you're either not quite sure what to do with or which are, even now, tucked away in your charity shop bag or your 'potential gifts for others' drawer because they're just not your thing. I do hope, though, that you didn't get any gifts which were so unwelcome that you'd have preferred the person to give you nothing at all.

That's where we find ourselves in our Malachi reading today. God is making an inventory of the gifts offered in the temple and has concluded that an empty temple and no offerings would be better than the gifts which have been brought for sacrifice.

This is a bleak moment, and it's all too easy to jump to the conclusion that God is saying that our worship isn't good enough, even that we aren't good enough. That's why it's important to remember that this is a message to the priests, not to individuals like you and me. The priests tended the animals used in the daily sacrifices at the temple, and they were supposed to bring the best of their flocks. But instead they would often sell the best to make money and bring the lower-value animals to the altar. This isn't God rejecting creatures that are imperfect; this is God being offended by priests who claim to honour God yet are really only interested in money and status.

God would rather have no gift at all than a gift given with ulterior motives, but God will always keep the doors wide open for gifts brought in sincerity and integrity, even if they're a bit wonky.

On this tenth day of Christmas, what gift would you like to give to God? It's hard to believe we can bring God joy by what we give, but we can. Why not ask what gift God would like from you?

LYNDALL BYWATER

The God who is always at work

'But my name is honoured by people of other nations from morning till night. All around the world they offer sweet incense and pure offerings in honour of my name. For my name is great among the nations,' says the Lord of Heaven's Armies. (v. 11, NLT)

It can be discouraging to discover that we're not indispensable. Have you ever been stood down from something because 'we don't really need you to be involved anymore' or 'we thought it would be good to give someone else a chance'? There's affirmation in being needed, isn't there? But if we're honest, there's also power in it, and it can be somewhat addictive.

Today's passage would have been a shocking message for the people of Israel. Written into the lore and traditions of their culture was the understanding that the God of creation was their God. They were the chosen people, and the only way for anyone to connect with their God was through them – through their priests, their worship rites and their law. Yet suddenly Malachi is telling them that there are people elsewhere in the world who are worshipping their God in totally different ways, without a Levite priest in sight, and that God is communing joyfully with them. How could the God of Israel find the worship of other races, tribes and religions acceptable?

The priests must have been devastated by this idea of God operating outside of their rules, but I find it rather reassuring. It's easy to get overwhelmed by the responsibilities of our faith – the call to live good lives, to demonstrate the love of God, to talk to friends, family, work colleagues and neighbours about Jesus. There's so much to do. How might it change our perspective if we call to mind the truth that God doesn't need us? God loves to partner with us in the work of salvation, but God doesn't grind to a halt when we don't show up, for whatever reason. God is continually at work all over the earth, drawing people into the embrace of love.

Have you ever been surprised to discover that God has been at work in someone's life without you realising it? Take time today to give thanks for the miracles you've seen which you didn't ask for and didn't expect.

LYNDALL BYWATER

Grace out of disgrace

'They passed on to the people the truth of the instructions they received from me. They did not lie or cheat; they walked with me, living good and righteous lives, and they turned many from lives of sin.' (v. 6, NLT)

Recently I was listening to the 1960s hit 'I saw her again' by The Mamas and the Papas. There's a point in the song when one of the singers comes in a couple of bars early, and I found myself wondering if it was a mistake or if it was meant to be like that. I consulted a knowledgeable friend who told me it had indeed been a mistake, but they'd decided to leave it in. Now it's one of the things which gives the song its character.

Our Malachi reading today continues God's criticism of the priests of Israel, and we will come back to that tomorrow, but today I want to take you on a detour to learn something about the Levites, because theirs is a remarkable story. Levi was one of the sons of Jacob, but he angered his father by behaving violently towards another tribe. As a result, when Jacob blessed his sons at the end of his life, he said that Levi's descendants would never inherit their own allotment of land in Israel. Fast-forward several hundred years and God is looking for a tribe to carry out the priestly duties in the tabernacle. The Levites get the job because they don't have their own land to look after, so they're free to give themselves to the care of God's house. Disgrace was turned into grace.

I imagine the singer in The Mamas and the Papas cringed every time he heard that misplaced entry, and yet the song would sound wrong without it. Are there things in your life which make you cringe, things that always feel like disgrace? Give it time, because I suspect you may find in years to come that God will turn those things into gifts of grace.

Is there a mistake (either yours or someone else's) which feels irredeemable? Hold that situation in prayer and remind yourself that you are held in the embrace of the one who can turn all things from disgrace into grace.

LYNDALL BYWATER

Faithful in the hidden things

'The man who hates and divorces his wife,' says the Lord, the God of Israel, 'does violence to the one he should protect,' says the Lord Almighty. So be on your guard, and do not be unfaithful. (v. 16, NIV)

When we think about spiritual heroes, it's easy to head straight for the big names who've impacted whole nations in powerful ways: John Wesley, William Booth, Martin Luther King Jr. In truth, the most heroic things I've ever seen are the quiet acts of care which have impacted just one or two people: time spent with loved ones in care homes; practical support offered to parents at the end of their tether; the smile or the kind word which lands at exactly the right moment. That is heroism indeed.

Malachi has some very challenging words to speak to the priests of his day. Priests were the leaders of God's people in those days, and they had immense power, which they were busy abusing. They were failing to teach the people how to live wholesome, holy lives, and when they did teach the things of God, they didn't practise what they preached. They were choosing not to apply the law fairly, living as though it was one rule for some and another for others. But the thing which seemed to offend God most was the way they were treating their wives. In Hebrew law, when you married a woman, she became entirely dependent on you for her well-being and her protection. To divorce her was to leave her entirely vulnerable, without home, income or safety. Of all the unfaithful actions these priests committed, God seemed to view this one as the worst, because it concerned the most vulnerable people in their lives.

It's reassuring to know that God doesn't measure our faithfulness by the nations we transform or the revivals we spark, isn't it? What counts is our commitment to the most vulnerable people around us. The faithfulness God most desires is our willingness to take care of those who need it most.

Who is God asking you to be faithful to today, and how can you live out that faithfulness to them? Remember, faithfulness isn't solving all the problems or meeting all the needs, it's doing what is yours to do today.

LYNDALL BYWATER

The clean-up

'At that time I will put you on trial. I am eager to witness against all sorcerers and adulterers and liars. I will speak against those who cheat employees of their wages, who oppress widows and orphans, or who deprive the foreigners living among you of justice, for these people do not fear me,' says the Lord of Heaven's Armies. (v. 5, NLT)

I've had four dogs, and they've divided themselves into two categories: those who love the post-walk clean-up and those who hate it. The process is the same for any dog – gently rubbing the coat with a towel to remove as much moisture as possible, then wiping the paws to make sure the mud doesn't get trailed through the house. But two of my dogs have hated every moment, trying to avoid it at all costs, whereas the other two have leaned into the process with joy, viewing it as something between a game and a spa treatment.

We're just over halfway through the book of Malachi and the judgements are over. God has made the case for the prosecution, and now the redemption is at hand. Today's passage is one of the many Old Testament pictures of Jesus. He's not named here as such, but you only have to recall him turning the tables over in the temple to know that he is the refiner's fire and the launderer's soap mentioned in verse 2 (see John 2:13–17). The Levite priests are going to be transformed, the temple is going to become the place of worship it was always meant to be, and the people are at last going to be treated fairly.

One of the greatest gifts God gives us is a good clean-up. The truth is that sometimes stuff gets stuck to us, from our own wrong choices or the wounds inflicted by others, which we just can't get rid of by ourselves. The only question is, will we be those who love the clean-up or will we try to avoid it at all costs? It can be an uncomfortable, even scary experience, but the one who cleanses us is love itself and does not change, therefore we will not be consumed.

Loving God, I welcome your cleansing today. Show me where I need forgiveness. Help me lean into the process of being made clean. I offer you my stains and scars, that you might wash me and heal me. Amen.

LYNDALL BYWATER

Getting unstuck

'Bring all the tithes into the storehouse so there will be enough food in my Temple. If you do… I will open the windows of heaven for you. I will pour out a blessing so great you won't have enough room to take it in!' (v. 10, NLT)

Have you ever boycotted something – chosen not to use or buy goods or services from a company, organisation or nation whose practices you disagree with? I remember boycotting a company for many years, then being surprised and a little embarrassed to discover that the issue I'd disapproved of so strongly had been resolved fairly quickly, only I'd forgotten to check! It's important to take a stance, but equally important not to get stuck in it.

Verse 10 of today's passage is perhaps the most famous in Malachi. How might we understand it more fully now that we've explored the background? Tithing in the Hebrew law was complex, but essentially it involved giving a tenth of your agricultural produce to the Levites – that tribe who took care of the temple and had no land of their own to support them. They in turn would give a tenth of what they received to the priests. (Not all the Levites were priests; they had all sorts of different roles in the temple.) What we know from today's reading is that lots of people had stopped giving their tithe. Maybe they just didn't want to; maybe they didn't trust the Levites because of the corruption we read about in Malachi 1—2. Whatever the reason, they seem to have been staging a boycott.

God calls them to change their stance and to stop withholding, but notice that this command comes after the promise of the clean-up. They're not being asked to overlook wrongdoing or prop up injustice. They're being invited to trust: to hear God's promise that things are changing and to step forward into a new era of justice and fruitfulness.

When we accept God's invitation to get unstuck and move forward, we discover a wealth of blessing we've never imagined before.

Are you stuck in a stance? Perhaps you took it up for good reasons, and you're not convinced anything has changed, but you know God is asking you to move on – to forgive and bring all that you've been withholding.

LYNDALL BYWATER

Together in prayer

Then those who honoured the Lord spoke with each other, and the Lord listened and heard them. The names of those who honoured the Lord and respected him were written in his presence in a book to be remembered. (v. 16, NCV)

I do like a chatty prayer meeting. I applaud you if you're one of those people who likes to get on with the praying rather than sitting around nattering, but I confess I'm one of those people who keeps starting yet another conversation when the leader is trying to get us all focused. I also confess that I've led prayer meetings where we didn't even get around to praying because we did so much talking! Malachi 3:16 is good news for people like me. It seems to suggest that God doesn't only listen to the prayer bit of the prayer meeting, but God listens to the chat as well.

Yesterday we reflected on Malachi's message about not getting stuck in old stances when God is doing a new thing. Today we meet a group of people who have felt something of the unfairness of life. They've watched as people bent on evil have thrived. Instead of staying stuck in their bitterness, they've come together to talk it over, and it's as though God has drawn up a chair, joined the circle and listened. They've been able to name those they feel have been mistreated, and God has made sure those names are recorded in heaven.

I think the reason I enjoy the chatty bit of prayer meetings is that it matters to me to know what's going on for the other people in the room. We may not be there to pray for our own issues, but when we connect as a community, sharing something of our joys and sorrows, our praying has a different dimension to it. Perhaps it's no wonder; God is community after all, so it makes sense that the Trinity would value our connections with one another just as much as our connection with them.

What a beautiful picture: Father, Son and Holy Spirit welcoming us into their conversation; us welcoming them into ours. Next time you feel bored or frustrated in a prayer meeting, call that image to mind and be encouraged.

LYNDALL BYWATER

Season change

But for you who revere my name the sun of righteousness shall rise, with healing in its wings. You shall go out leaping like calves from the stall. (v. 2, NRSV)

I was chatting with a friend of mine recently and she asked me a question about a conversation we'd been having on WhatsApp about a year ago. WhatsApp has a handy date-search function, allowing you to look back at the messages you exchanged with a particular person on any given day, so I went back to read what we'd said. An hour later I realised I'd been completely absorbed in that year-old conversation, mostly because I'd been marvelling at how much had happened in both our lives since then. It was a joyful reminder that the struggles we go through will always come to an end and that the goodness of God is eternal.

As we walk through the wintery days of January, today's passage comes as something of a tonic, doesn't it? It's a reminder that the sun will rise and that we will feel its warmth again. The image of calves being released from the stall is a reminder that spring will come. After all the judgements Malachi has had to deliver, this message of healing and new life must have come as a great relief.

The last few words of verse 3 tell us that these wonderful things will happen on the day when God acts. That's a helpful reminder that we can't make these season changes happen for ourselves. Our times are in God's hands. God will eventually eradicate every evil and injustice, cutting it out at the root, so it can't grow again. God will bring the spring; God will spread healing wings of love over us; God will set us free from the things that hem us in; and God will fill us with so much abundant life that we can't help but leap for joy.

Keep an eye out for those first spring flowers – the snowdrops and crocuses that arrive even when winter's still in full swing. Take a photo of one to serve as a reminder that God is going to act.

LYNDALL BYWATER

17

From generation to generation

He will turn the hearts of parents to their children and the hearts of children to their parents, so that I will not come and strike the land with a curse. (v. 6, NRSV)

Malachi Justin was five years old when his first baby tooth fell out. He got the princely sum of £5 from the tooth fairy and was so troubled by the idea of people having to sleep on the street that he gave it to The Salvation Army in Ilford, with a note asking them to use it to help homeless people. The Salvation Army responded by using that £5 donation as the start of a fundraising campaign to build pop-up housing for rough sleepers. Five years and £5 million later, the new centre opened, providing accommodation for 42 homeless people, and its name is Malachi Place.

As we reach the end of the Old Testament, the words we find aren't about keeping laws or making sacrifices, they're about children and families. Perhaps that's because, when injustice and disaffection permeate a society, they fracture it. Families split over politics, and generations turn against each other because they see the world in such different ways. It matters to God that the priests be challenged and the worshipping practices of the people be set right, but it matters far more that the people come together again in one loving community.

Notice that the parents' hearts turn towards the children before the children's hearts turn towards the parents. The initiative must come from us, the adults. Children have wisdom which we need to hear, even if they sometimes feel like an alien race, so different are their perspectives. Malachi Place was born because some adults turned their ears and their hearts towards a little child. As we step into the New Testament, we find ourselves at the birth of another little child. May we have the humility to turn our hearts towards the younger generation, that we may hear God's word through them.

Is there a child in your life who you could commit to pray for this year? If you can spend time with them, make an effort to listen to them and to notice the wisdom they bring.

LYNDALL BYWATER

Ephesians: images of the church

Liz Hogarth writes…

I visited Paris last year and my daughter wanted to go to the Eiffel Tower. When we got there, we were glad we had booked in advance as there were crowds of people waiting to go up. Once at the top, I looked out and was struck by just how many people were going about their business below and how many of them probably didn't have much interest in God. The task of reaching people with the gospel can seem immense, but the church, the body of Christ, is there to make that possible.

Written about AD60, the letter to the church at Ephesus was penned from Rome during Paul's imprisonment. It was not intended to confront any heresy or problem, but was sent with Tychicus, a messenger from Ephesus, to strengthen, encourage and explain the nature and purpose of the church. Several pictures of the church are presented: body, temple, mystery, new self, bride and soldier. All these images illustrate how we need to work together to achieve a common goal. The question of unity is therefore central to this letter. There is a call to look at our own lives and put a stop to the things that may cause disunity, such as being overly critical of leaders or gossiping.

That said, in the present day, all sorts of churches and gatherings of Christians are available for us to join. So, a broader unity is possible, while holding sometimes very differing views.

The church at Ephesus was established in AD53 on Paul's homeward journey to Jerusalem and was one of the more important of the new Gentile congregations. Being a Christian in the first century was a difficult, indeed dangerous, thing. New believers were probably challenged daily by neighbours, friends, family and the authorities. Their churches would have been places of refuge from the hazardous world outside, but also places where they could draw strength.

Perhaps we should see the whole of Ephesians as a refuelling stop, a demonstration, or bird's eye view, of how to effectively be the body of Christ, before we turn our faces outwards to bring the gospel to the wider world.

All shapes and sizes

Make every effort to keep the unity of the Spirit through the bond of peace. There is one body and one Spirit… one Lord, one faith, one baptism; one God and Father of all, who is over all and through all and in all. (NIV)

One of the most significant roles of the Holy Spirit is to build unity. The Spirit leads us in this, but we also have to do our bit in keeping the peace. So often Christians can be divided over really small things. I can recall arguments at various churches over types of chairs in the sanctuary, the demise of the organ and paint colours for various rooms. We can also differ on important matters. If we focus on God and not on ourselves, then it helps us to keep the peace, both on the important issues and those that are less important. These verses from Ephesians challenge us to see all shapes and sizes of Christian congregations as part of one body.

My work has taken me to all sorts of different churches both in this country and overseas. I've seen worship that involved dancing in the aisles, burning incense, waving flags, trained choirs and extremely loud guitar-led bands. In some of these churches, the priest or minister wore flowing robes, in others, a suit, and on one occasion, at a lively worship service in Australia, shorts and a T-shirt.

Humility is paramount here. Our lives need to express our belief that the body of Christ is one. It is important to affirm our love for other believers, even for those with whom we differ, rather than focus on our differences.

Verse 6 talks about God 'over all' and this shows his overruling care or transcendence, but he is also 'through all and in all', therefore very much present in our world and in the actions and lives of believers. This is called immanence. It is important to recognise that God is both transcendent and immanent. Both are reassuring.

Give thanks that God is both 'over all' and 'in all'. Think of a Christian congregation that is different from your own and pray for them and their work and witness.

LIZ HOGARTH

A supporting role

From him the whole body, joined and held together by every supporting ligament, grows and builds itself up in love, as each part does its work. (NIV)

At one point in my career, I was working in a very junior role at a Christian charity. I was part of a team who had organised for the well-known author and speaker R.T. Kendall to come and address them. As the most junior member of the team, I was charged with waiting outside to watch for his car and then to run in and tell my boss he had arrived. I did this but was a bit slow identifying the Revd Kendall, and he spotted me waiting.

It seemed rude to rush away, so I showed him and his companion into the building, while busily explaining that I needed to go and get my boss. I was completely taken aback when he said that he would like to sit down and chat to me first. Looking back on it, I think he realised that I was trying to efface myself due to lack of confidence. Finally, I persuaded him that I did really need to alert my boss to his presence in the building. After that it was business as usual, except that I walked taller from having been singled out by the guest speaker.

I mention this because as a very junior member of the team that day I was definitely a 'supporting ligament'. In church life most of us are 'supporting ligaments' and maybe we don't value ourselves or our roles very highly, but Paul is clearly saying that we are all needed and play a role in building up the body in love.

Often those who serve in the background don't get a lot of thanks or notice for what they do, but just occasionally, like R.T. Kendall that day, someone does pay attention and singles out a 'supporting ligament' for a bit of notice and appreciation.

Think about someone in your church who serves faithfully in ways that are not high profile. Pray for them, and if it's within your remit, show them some appreciation for what they do this week.

LIZ HOGARTH

God's dwelling place

In him the whole building is joined together and rises to become a holy temple in the Lord. And in him you too are being built together to become a dwelling in which God lives by his Spirit. (vv. 21–22, NIV)

Paul announces that Gentiles and Jews are now part of the same family. This was radical teaching at the time, as was the notion that the temple was made up of human beings rather than being the physical building in Jerusalem.

In these final verses of Paul's temple vision, he talks about how Christians are being changed and renewed to be a receptacle in which God lives by his Spirit. Perhaps we don't think very highly of ourselves at times, maybe we don't much like our bodies, particularly as we get older, but by the power of his Spirit God makes his home with us and uses us – every bit of us, our imperfect bodies and our sometimes fragile and easily distracted minds.

I heard the phrase 'just bodies' recently in relation to a discussion on sexual purity, but we are so much more than 'just bodies'. We are God's craftsmanship, made in his image, his dwelling place. It matters terribly to God, and ultimately to us, what we do with them. I think it's only when we understand God's perspective that we can also understand that we are not being asked to follow a set of rules when it comes to morality, but to honour the receptacle in which 'God lives by his Spirit'.

Someone once commented that we need to understand more deeply that God dwells in us. We don't need to ask him to show up at a worship service, for instance, because, as Christians, if we are there, he is there too. This thought has made a big difference to me. I now feel more confident walking into a room on my own as I know that God is there with me.

Pray for someone who you think would find it hard to accept that God wants to make his home with them and use them to his glory.

LIZ HOGARTH

Making God's wisdom known

His intent was that now, through the church, the manifold wisdom of God should be made known to the rulers and authorities in the heavenly realms. (v. 10, NIV)

The heart of this passage contains one of the most important reasons given in the Bible for the church's existence. We are called to be the means through which angels and heavenly beings can see the wisdom of God's redemption plan for his creation. Paul tells us that God's plan was always to make himself known to everyone, not just to the Jews, but this had been kept hidden (v. 9). Now, through his church, the full extent of God's plan is revealed. Our conduct is therefore very important. When the angels see the church serving and glorifying God, they see God's plan coming to fruition and they worship him.

Being part of a church should be a fantastic way to tap into all the wonderful wealth and glory and freedom to be found in Christ. However, sadly for many people this is not what happens. All too often, we just sit there waiting to be fed. Perhaps we forget what Paul talks about later in this passage, that one of the chief riches we have is our free and confident access to God (v. 12). This is not a God who is uninterested, changeable or cross, but a loving Father ready to listen to us.

One of the most puzzling aspects of this passage is why Paul describes his sufferings as the glory of the Ephesian believers. Commentators suggest he is encouraging them to understand that his being thrown into prison proves that the Christian way is working, as it has prompted a reaction from both rulers on this earth and the powers of darkness. They should therefore rejoice.

There is a challenge here: are our churches today posing a threat to the powers of darkness? The early Christians had passion for their cause, and maybe we need to reignite that passion.

---

*There are many Christians around the world who are persecuted for their faith. Open Doors (**opendoorsuk.org**) has some good prompts for prayer.*

LIZ HOGARTH

Significantly different

You were taught, with regard to your former way of life, to put off your old self, which is being corrupted by its deceitful desires; to be made new in the attitude of your minds; and to put on the new self, created to be like God in true righteousness and holiness. (vv. 22–24, NIV)

Paul's command is to put on the 'new self', to turn our backs on our old ways and to follow Christ's example. However, as we know all too well, we don't automatically express all the right thoughts and feelings when we become Christians.

There will be stumbles, but, as we listen to God, we will be changing from month to month and year to year. This goes right back to Jesus' teaching in the gospels, which stress that our hearts and minds need to be right and from there, albeit sometimes slowly, change will come.

Being a new creation, or putting on the new self, is wonderfully freeing and full of hope. I became a Christian at 19, but even at that young age I felt I had a lot of baggage and was stuck with what I had accumulated. In time, I discovered this was not true and it was possible to start afresh and put on a new self. Others around us may take time to truly appreciate that we have changed, but God will see it.

One change that surprised me when I was a new Christian was that people started to confide in and bring their problems to me. I looked the same, but perhaps, in the past, I had projected something that implied I wouldn't be sympathetic or patient with weakness. The new self was seeping out, almost unbidden. It can be a challenge to see people differently, but we should encourage each other by continually looking for signs that we are being changed by God, whether we have been Christians for 40 minutes or 40 years.

Give thanks that God is at work in your life. Thinking about your experience as a Christian so far, are you conscious of changes for the better in your thoughts, attitudes and actions?

LIZ HOGARTH

The bride of Christ

Husbands, love your wives, just as Christ loved the church and gave himself up for her to make her holy, cleansing her by the washing with water through the word, and to present her to himself as a radiant church. (vv. 25–27, NIV)

Paul holds marriage in high regard. It is a holy union, requiring unselfish care for each other. The love a husband has for his wife should be the love of self-sacrifice, a love that seeks the highest love of others. The creation story tells of God's plan that husband and wife should be one (Genesis 2:24), and Jesus also referred to this plan (Matthew 19:5). Much has been written about Paul's teaching on relationships from this passage, but our focus today is on what we can learn about the nature and purpose of the church.

Paul uses the intimacy of marriage to describe how close Christ is to the church. In the same way that a man and woman become one flesh, Christ and his church are one. The relationship springs from the love and sacrifice of Christ. He has lovingly chosen the church to be his bride (v. 25), he provides and cares for his bride (v. 29) and the church's response is to be faithful to him (v. 24).

We also see that the church's response should be to care for and submit to each other (v. 21). Love and service should be the defining features of the church. My son is currently away on a Christian youth camp and each day we have been asked to pray that God will raise up a new generation of Christian leaders, teachers and pastors for his church. The sacrifice of the leaders who have taken these young people away for a week in tents – mostly in the rain and wind this year – should be applauded, as it is done for the sake of the church. What examples come to mind when you think about serving the body of Christ?

'Love each other. Just as I have loved you, you should love each other. Your love for one another will prove to the world that you are my disciples' (John 13:34–35, NLT).

LIZ HOGARTH

Soldiers ready for battle

Stand firm then, with the belt of truth buckled round your waist, with the breastplate of righteousness in place, and with your feet fitted with the readiness that comes from the gospel of peace. (vv. 14–15, NIV)

I suspect I am not alone in having acted out putting on the different pieces of armour in Sunday school. I understood they were about spiritual warfare, but it was only when a friend, who was going through a very difficult divorce, told me how she would repeat these verses first thing each morning and mentally put on the belt, breastplate, shoes, shield, helmet and sword, that their importance really hit home. She told me how putting on the armour gave her the strength to face whatever was coming round the corner that day.

Since then, I've tried to be more mindful about putting on the armour. I've found it helpful to think about how the breastplate of righteousness protects my emotions and sense of self-worth as I remind myself that God sent his Son to die for me. I think of the shoes as enabling me to step out in the assurance that God is with me and empowers me to take the good news to others. I imagine the shield of faith protecting me from setbacks that could steal my hope and the helmet of salvation stopping me from doubting God and what Jesus has done for me. Finally, I take up the only offensive weapon on the list, the sword of the Spirit, because there are times when I need to confront Satan's schemes and trust in the truth of God's word.

Like soldiers in a war who are often not aware of what is happening in the other theatres of conflict, we do not always appreciate the struggles of those around us, but we are each called to play our part and defend what is right and what is true, on that piece of ground where God has placed us.

If you are feeling under pressure, imagine putting on each piece of God's armour. Pray as you do so and ask for his strength to face the day.

LIZ HOGARTH

The gift of creativity

Catherine Larner writes…

Like many people I have always enjoyed making things – cooking, sewing, knitting – but always within boundaries. I followed patterns and recipes, completed tapestry kits and wrote articles for magazine commissions. There wasn't much room for play or expression, for innovation or experimentation. For me, that meant I never felt truly creative. To be so felt risky, indulgent and wasteful – things were likely to go wrong!

One day I attended a creative writing session organised as part of a weekend of activities at my church. The leader was known to me as a children's author who lived in the town, and I was rather in awe of her.

The course was many years ago now, but I have always remembered how she began by reminding us that as we believe in a creator God and accept that we are made in his likeness, it means we have the gift of creativity too. Whether we are painters, designers, writers, musicians or none of these things, we all have some level of creativity since we are made in the image of God. It means we can, and should, create because it's part of who we are.

In that session something clicked inside me. My desire to invent, imagine, problem-solve and embellish was acceptable, permissible and pleasing to God.

What's more, thinking creatively and expressing myself in new ways need not be a selfish pleasure. Though I gain delight and fulfilment in reflecting something of my wonder of God's creation, in doing so I might also be communicating my faith to others. By engaging in creative prayer, reading and worship, I might deepen my relationship with God and allow both myself and others to experience God more fully.

So, what does the Bible tell us about how we might do this? Are there examples of creative practices and creative people to follow? What does God have to say about being creative? Let's explore together.

Space and time

'Truly I tell you, anyone who will not receive the kingdom of God like a little child will never enter it.' (v. 15, NIV)

There's something about being told to 'be creative'. Whenever I've gone on a course or workshop to try something new, instead of feeling liberated to experiment, I've clammed up. The burst of activity from those around me, the time commitment, the leader judging and evaluating – it has all felt as though I've had to fulfil a task instead of releasing new skills and opportunities.

At work, in our personal lives, even in church, there seems to be a constant pressure to deliver and perform. So the invitation to 'be creative' can feel like yet another obligation to add to the seemingly endless list of things we are expected to achieve or qualities we should possess.

However, being creative does not need to be about delivering results. We don't need to think about the outcome or the audience for our act of creativity. We are urged to come to Christ with the trust and innocence of a child, with no preconceptions or expectations, and with all the freedom, joy and playfulness of creative expression.

It may feel as though life has conditioned us out of those qualities, but we can invite them in once again. The poet Mary Oliver calls moments like this 'not thinking, not remembering and not wanting'.

If we can, let's put aside our commitments and obligations, our hopes and expectations for a while. We might like to go for a walk, spend time in a garden, sit by a window or open our Bible, and then, enjoying the moment and seeking the presence of God, let's daydream, doodle, wonder and wander.

Just like a child, we should delight in the here and now and, by so doing, we'll find ourselves more energised and enlivened, and our ability and ideas will flourish.

Put away your phone, sit quietly in a place you feel most comfortable or take a walk. Invite the Lord to speak to you and see what happens.

CATHERINE LARNER

A blank canvas

In the beginning God created the heavens and the earth. Now the earth was formless and empty, darkness was over the surface of the deep, and the Spirit of God was hovering over the waters. (v. 1, NIV)

In the beginning there was nothing: a blank canvas, an empty sheet of paper, silence.

If ever you've taken that leap of starting to write a story, paint a picture or compose a piece of music, you'll know that the first act is the hardest. Where do you begin? It's likely that you won't have everything in place as you start and fleshing out that initial idea will involve editing, rubbing out or hitting a few bad notes before everything comes together.

Amazingly, God knew what was needed from the first day and everything he created was perfect, stunning and extraordinary. He spoke and it came into being. Day by day more appeared: the stars in the sky, huge mountain peaks, the deep, deep oceans. He created vast landscapes and minute organisms, all intricately fashioned, all taking their place in the big picture of his universe. He didn't make an environment which merely sustained life, he formed something which was extravagant, splendid and magnificent. And he worked at it. Day by day we hear that God spoke, saw, named and made. He is mentioned 30 times throughout Genesis 1.

God created the world, in all its glory, in extraordinary detail. When he spoke, he showed his ingenuity and flair, his inventiveness and his generosity. His creation draws people to the divine (Romans 1:20).

I've often met people who are wavering or without faith, and they say how they wonder at the natural world. When they've taken time to look at the sunset, the waterfall, the rainbow, they say they are stopped short. How can this world have come into being without some powerful, extraordinary, flamboyant God?

Lord, I want to walk with you today and look around to notice your creation, the colour of the sky, the sense of the breeze, the texture of the tree trunk. Thank you for the wonders of all you have made. Amen.

CATHERINE LARNER

In his likeness

So God created mankind in his own image, in the image of God he created them; male and female he created them.' (v. 27, NIV)

God made us in his likeness, reflecting his nature mentally, morally and socially and setting us apart from other creatures in how we experience truth, beauty, meaning and will.

Like our creator God, we too have a skill and desire for creativity and invention. It is part of what makes us human. It's a blessing, a calling and a responsibility to be creative. We are required to bring order to our society and our world. As God made the world from nothing, so we are called to create something out of what exists.

Some of us will interpret creativity as artistic. Many of my friends who work in science, medicine and administration have told me that they don't consider themselves creative. However, to create means bringing something into existence which wasn't there before; that could be a meal, a conversation, a letter to a friend, a beautiful garden or the solution to a problem.

Recently Rick Rubin, the American music producer, wrote a book proclaiming his manifesto on creativity – *The Creative Act: A way of being* (Canongate Books, 2023). It topped the bestseller charts for weeks, signalling how much interest there is in the subject. 'Creativity is not a rare ability,' he writes. It is 'a fundamental aspect of being human. It's our birthright. And it's for all of us.'

Rick is known for his unorthodox ways of working with his clients. Instead of advising them, he makes a space for them to return to the place of innocence and naivety from where they first made music. He says that our creativity isn't about our output or the recognition we might receive.

I've found it helpful to think about the Lord similarly giving me permission to be free to play with my writing, to stop striving and seeking to see results but to enjoy the process and to offer it to God as an act of worship.

Heavenly Father, thank you for giving me the gift of creativity. Help me to explore the skills you have given me, not for any end goal, but simply to enjoy spending time with you, getting to know you more deeply. Amen.

CATHERINE LARNER

Something new

Do not conform to the pattern of this world, but be transformed by the renewing of your mind. (v. 2, NIV)

For a number of years, I worked as a magazine editor. I was responsible for filling the pages with news and feature articles each month. It meant commissioning writers to report on recent developments but also covering topics regularly mentioned, season by season. I had to build a well-balanced, attractive magazine, finding fresh ways of making familiar subjects exciting and stimulating.

I didn't really consider myself creative at the time. I was frustrated that I couldn't write the articles myself, thinking that writing was a more interesting, fulfilling, valuable (and valued) use of my skills, experience and time. Looking back, I can see that being an editor is a privileged and important role, and I found it rewarding coming up with new ideas, although I didn't realise it fully at the time.

I have a friend who works in an administrative role in a business. She knows people who are artists or who have hobbies in textiles and print-making. She doesn't see herself as creative because neither her job nor her leisure time is spent making things. However, she displays great creativity in her work through building relationships, seeing new ways of presenting information and in recognising where to invest time and resources to the benefit of the organisation. Having an inventive, creative mind is valuable in all aspects of our lives and society.

In his book *Finding the Peacemakers* (Hodder and Stoughton, 2022), Dan Morrice talks about the situation in Israel and Palestine. In recent times we've seen terrible conflict, but Morrice visited the area some years ago and met people who were looking for ways to solve disagreements and opposition creatively. Being creative isn't just about craft or making things; it is about finding solutions or gaining a new perspective. What could be more creative than bringing people together, building relationships and forging a spirit of hope and community?

Lord, please give me your wisdom and insight to approach situations with fresh eyes, mind and heart. I pray for courage and conviction to speak and to act, to bring your spirit of peace, hope and forgiveness wherever I am. Amen.
                                                              CATHERINE LARNER

Colours and talents

He has filled them with skill to do all kinds of work as engravers, designers, embroiderers in blue, purple and scarlet yarn and fine linen, and weavers – all of them skilled workers and designers. (v. 35, NIV)

For those of us who are artists or makers and think we are not contributing to the Lord's work, this is a beautiful and encouraging passage. Look at the vibrant colours, the quality of the materials, the flamboyance of what is being made and the variety of craftspeople listed! They had been given these skills and talents by God and they were working to clear and detailed specifications given by the Lord himself in the building of his tabernacle.

This book of the Bible is one that Cambridgeshire florist Cecilia says she turns to time and again in her work. A few years ago, having enjoyed creating the flower arrangements for a family wedding, she decided to leave her job in PR to become a florist.

'I was so excited by the creative process,' she says. 'There are endless possibilities of colour combination, movement, design and texture, and the power of flowers to express so many things.'

Speaking to the London Institute of Contemporary Christianity (LICC), she described the joy and satisfaction she feels working with the colours and shapes of the flowers and plants. She thinks that using the gift of creativity is 'a balm for the soul' but recognises that her work is also an act of prayer and meditation as she picks the plants and moulds her displays.

She says: 'I believe we have a creator God and that we all have the potential to be creative. I try to use this creativity to bring joy and blessing to others for his glory. It is a way of understanding ourselves and our world more deeply, of communicating better and sharing together… I receive this gift of floristry with thanksgiving and try to use it in worship of him every day.' You can read the full interview here: **licc.org.uk/florist**.

Show me, Lord, how to use my creativity to get closer to you and to celebrate the talents you have given me. Help me to recognise where my creative gifts can serve your greater purpose and bring joy and blessing to others. Amen.

CATHERINE LARNER

Flair and flourish

Do you see someone skilled in their work? They will serve before kings; they will not serve before officials of low rank. (v. 29, NIV)

These days creativity is a buzz word both in the workplace and in society generally. Though most of us still tend to think of creativity in the arts, it is also now viewed as the skill of the future, a way for businesses to step away from the crowd. It signals innovation and success.

There is also a recognition of how we can personally gain fulfilment and satisfaction from being creative. Books about thinking creatively regularly top the bestseller charts, and classes and courses exploring creativity are oversubscribed. For some employers, educational achievements and life experience are no longer key requirements of potential candidates; instead they look for the ability to 'think outside the box'.

Creativity is as much an act of labour or work as anything else, and it is a process of growth. We often think of creative people waiting for inspiration, needing to be struck by a muse in order to produce a painting, song or story. More commonly, though, they work at finding the solution.

The author of 'The Chronicles of Narnia' series, C.S. Lewis, was a writer, scholar and theologian, prolific in his output. In addition to these children's books, he produced devotional works, science fiction novels and was also a gifted and inspiring lecturer at the University of Oxford. When he had an idea for a story, he was known to write it in many different forms to see which genre would best suit it. He wrote some stories first as a poem and then as a play before deciding how they should finally appear. He worked at it, but he also pondered an idea for many years before bringing it to fruition. Creativity isn't all about play but about doing the very best that we can.

Lord, help me today to work for your glory. I want to do it to the best of my ability, and I want my efforts to honour you. Amen.

CATHERINE LARNER

Telling a story

But Jesus bent down and started to write on the ground with his finger. (v. 6, NIV)

Jesus was teaching in the temple courts when the religious leaders, seeking to discredit him as a man of God, led him into a trap. They brought a woman to him who had been caught in adultery. The law stated she should be stoned. What would Jesus do?

In this moment of huge emotion and confrontation, Jesus took a moment of quiet – and doodled. We don't know what he drew. It could have been a picture, a word or a pattern. Some have suggested that Jesus may have written other sins here – pride, lust, envy, false witness. Perhaps Jesus was scribbling in the dirt as a distraction, averting his eyes. Whatever lay behind it, his action shows that Jesus saw the value of doing something new and surprising, and something active, too. We don't just see him looking into the distance; he was making a mark on the ground.

This creative act helped Jesus, momentarily, to step outside the situation, and it signalled that he was thinking and acting differently from how people expected him to behave and speak.

A creative activity can help give our minds a break from the demands of everyday life, and it can also help reduce stress levels and bring about a sense of calm and well-being. A few years ago, there was a trend in adult colouring books for just that reason.

We don't need to have a goal in our creativity. The act of focusing on something we enjoy is enough. Perhaps it is an opportunity to think, to meditate, to talk to or listen to God.

Write this verse on a sheet of paper and let your pencil run freely, embellishing the words or shading your lines. Listen to what God might be saying to you about this passage.

CATHERINE LARNER

Modelled by Christ

For we are God's handiwork, created in Christ Jesus to do good works, which God prepared in advance for us to do. (v. 10, NIV)

Here we are again reminded of how we are intricately and wonderfully made in the image of God, possessing his characteristics, reflecting his glory and being equipped to do his work.

We're also told that God has a plan for each one of us. We don't need to copy what anyone else is doing, neither do we need to compare ourselves with others. We are unique, special and singular, and God loves us for who we are in him.

We don't need to do good works to be accepted by God, but he would like us to share all that he has done for us. Consider how Jesus engaged with others. Throughout his life we see many instances of how he applied his creative nature to teaching and ministry, mentoring and relationships. Jesus was skilled in communicating – inspiring and encouraging one person, leading and motivating a team, engaging and enthusing a crowd and telling a good story. He was also a carpenter, a craftsman. He could take a rough plank of timber and shape it into a useful and beautiful piece of furniture. Even as he was known for sharing the message of his father's love for us, so the objects he built would also have shown elements of his character. He would have shown integrity in fulfilling each job well and to an agreed price and time.

Each job would also have given him an opportunity to talk to the people engaging him in the work. Everyday tasks or conversations could be brought round to issues of eternity as people became curious about what motivated him in his life and work.

We can use our creativity to find ways to communicate our story, whether overtly sharing our faith when witnessing to friends or acquaintances or simply showing the wider world who we are and what is important to us.

Heavenly Father, I want to follow Jesus' example in communicating my faith to others in engaging and creative ways, but I also pray that my love of you will shine through everything I do today, in both actions and words. Amen.

CATHERINE LARNER

Creativity of fellow Christians

The heavens declare the glory of God; the skies proclaim the work of his hands. (v. 1, NIV)

Just as God's creation reflects and announces his glory to all the world, so the output of our hands and minds can honour and celebrate our Lord. We may not bring into being the heavens and the earth, but we can offer stories, paintings or music to praise his name.

Magnificent churches and cathedrals and fine art have presented the immense creativity of believers over the generations as they have sought to express their faith. Ornate altarpieces, soaring organ music, stained-glass windows illuminated by sunlight, vast friezes depicting scenes of the holy story – these lift our spirits and remind us of the ethereal, transcendent presence of our God.

This continues today as we see Christian communities work together on lavish and detailed needlework, worship leaders compose songs, artists form poignant sculptures and craftspeople shape stone and wood for furnishings and decoration. Believers continue to bring something of the wonder of God through the labour of their hands and the expression of their imagination, challenging and inspiring us with their creations.

Art doesn't have to proclaim the gospel explicitly, though. The artist Charlie Mackesy has achieved international success through his simple and moving illustrated story *The Boy, The Mole, The Fox and The Horse* (Harper Collins, 2019), in which he reminds readers of the importance of kindness.

J.R.R. Tolkien wanted his books to depict the struggle of good and evil. *The Hobbit* and *The Lord of the Rings* trilogy have had a huge impact as classics of literature and more recently as films. He saw his creativity as a 'supreme gift' from God, and he labelled himself a 'sub-creator', emulating God's creation through his own work.

An authentic expression of a believer can be a powerful reflection of the glory of God and can bring us to a closer understanding of the nature of his being.

Do something creative today. Ask God to bless your hands, mind and heart as you begin. Write a song of worship, meditate while you knit or sew, make bread or mould a lump of clay as you remember a Bible passage.

CATHERINE LARNER

Creative praise

Praise him with the sounding of the trumpet, praise him with the harp and lyre, praise him with tambourine and dancing. (vv. 3–4, NIV)

As created and creative beings, part of our purpose is to capture what is on God's heart and to sing it, paint it, build it, sew it or write it! Throughout the Bible, we read about creative people who used their God-given skills, gifts and ingenuity to worship God and serve others.

When God said he was going to flood the earth, he gave Noah instructions to build an ark to save the animals and his family. Noah wasn't an architect, carpenter or construction worker, but God equipped Noah to do it (Genesis 6:9–22). God gave Moses the measurements for building the tabernacle and sent his Holy Spirit to fill Bezalel and Oholiab 'with wisdom, with understanding, with knowledge and with all kinds of skills… to engage in all kinds of crafts' (Exodus 31:3, 5) to make it beautiful.

David played music and wrote songs praising God and bringing joy, but he also knew how to calm and soothe King Saul with the gentle sound of the lyre (1 Samuel 16:14–23). David also expressed his sorrow and despair in the Psalms, which still provide comfort and solace today.

Solomon wrote proverbs and poetry. He can also be credited with creative problem-solving, as he was called on to decide who was the true mother when two women both claimed a baby was theirs (1 Kings 3:16–28).

We read of other people in the Bible who used their skills to further the kingdom. Paul, Priscilla and Aquilla worked as tentmakers to earn money to be able to go out and spread the gospel. Tabitha made clothing for the poor. Ezra and Nehemiah rebuilt the temple and the walls around Jerusalem.

We can all use our creativity for God's glory. When we use our gifts for the good of others, we honour God.

Do you have skills that come so naturally that you don't think anything of them? Think about how this might be a gift from God which you could use more fully and more creatively.

CATHERINE LARNER

Coming close to God

I will sing to the Lord all my life; I will sing praise to my God as long as I live. (v. 33, NIV)

Our world is full of machinery, industry and technology, and we sometimes forget to enjoy the natural environment God created or to respond to our own inherent creative spirit. There are also times when we just don't feel particularly creative. Does this diminish who we are in Christ? Are we squandering our talents if we don't explore our creativity?

I have a friend who was particularly gifted as a manager and as a medical practitioner. She recently retired and was looking forward to being creative now that her time was her own. She had never pursued any hobbies or activities in her leisure time and, as she signed up for workshops and courses, she gradually realised that she didn't have a natural aptitude for the pottery, sewing or painting that she had so admired in others.

She thought this would be a new chapter in her life when she would devote herself to creative activities with the same singlemindedness and success that she had in her practical and scientific roles in the past; but she eventually came to find her value and role in serving others again. Her particular creative gifting was in problem-solving and leadership, and she was able to use those gifts through volunteering with local charities.

We are uniquely and wonderfully made, and what might be one person's strength and gifting may not be another's.

There's a saying: 'He who sings well, prays twice.' Our creative expression, whatever that may be, adds to our act of prayer and worship. We can use our God-given abilities to share the gospel and help transform lives. Our relationships, work, leisure time and faith are all enhanced by our creativity.

Lord, I don't want to make something just to achieve and produce, but to serve you and to spread your word. Help me to see my giftings through your eyes. Amen.

CATHERINE LARNER

Putting ourselves in the picture

All scripture is God-breathed and is useful for teaching, rebuking, correcting and training in righteousness, so that the servant of God may be thoroughly equipped for every good work. (v. 16, NIV)

The Bible tells us how God has worked in and through his people over the generations. It is a divinely inspired book, which teaches us about who God is. It is our manual for living, and we study, ponder and interrogate the Bible so that we might know the heart of God.

A few years ago, I tried something different and began using *lectio divina*, an ancient monastic practice which involves an imaginative engagement with the scriptures.

For example, taking the passage about Jesus calming the storm (Matthew 8:23–27), I first pray that the Holy Spirit will give me an insight, and then I read the story slowly two or three times and once aloud. Following this I pause to reflect on what the scripture is saying to me personally. I picture myself as a witness, a bystander or even a participant in the scene, and consider how this makes me feel.

I might imagine the waves smashing into the boat, threatening to knock me over. I see myself drenched and terrified. The boat is going to capsize, and Jesus isn't even awake. Does he care what I'm going through? Then I talk to God, I tell him how I feel. I wait and listen.

This isn't how I was brought up with the Bible. We were encouraged to listen to a sermon, read a commentary or attend a house group discussion, but I have found it very powerful to imagine myself in a scene with Jesus. It has given me new insights and raised questions or answers that are not always so apparent in a normal reading.

Engaging our imagination calls to our creativity and invites us to draw closer to God. It took me to a much deeper understanding and response to the passage than I had before.

Thank you, Lord, for the riches of your word – for the poetry, the prophecy, the history, the law. Please bless me and lead me in my reading of it, allowing it to transform me. Amen.

CATHERINE LARNER

We each have gifts

We have different gifts, according to the grace given to each of us. If your gift is prophesying, then prophesy in accordance with your faith; if it serving, then serve; if it is teaching, then teach. (vv. 6–7, NIV)

We need to be God's messengers in all aspects of society – art, politics, education, finance, entertainment – bringing salt and light and showing something of God's presence in all its wonder and splendour. Many people will not seek out a church building or want to hear a sermon, but they may be touched by beautiful music, feel they are taken out of themselves through a stunning piece of artwork or empathise with another person's situation through a novel.

We should consider how our creative thinking, skills and actions might help us to spread the gospel. That might involve making a piece of art which illustrates God's goodness, or it might be creatively witnessing to friends, family or colleagues.

I remember inviting a work colleague to a church meeting some years ago. She had been asking questions about the Christian message and wanted to know more but had been wary of attending a church service. I suggested that she approach the meeting as she would a work conference. I would introduce her to God, through explaining the teaching and readings, and then she could spend time in his presence, getting to know him before deciding if she felt able to call him her friend. Sometimes by presenting our story differently we can make it more accessible to someone.

The parables are our example in this. They are perfectly crafted, timeless stories which are incredibly concise and deceptively simple but are loaded with meaning and significance. They encourage us to engage, think and respond, and have a much greater impact than if their message was delivered as a sermon.

Heavenly Father, help me to recognise my particular gifts, to enjoy them and to find new and powerful ways of spreading your word through my own creativity. Amen.

CATHERINE LARNER

We are a new creation

Therefore, if anyone is in Christ, the new creation has come: the old has gone, the new is here! (v. 17, NIV)

God created a perfect world which, even though it was corrupted through the fall of Adam and Eve, still possesses infinite beauty, complexity and synchronicity. God wanted us to experience life in its fullness, though, so he gave us the opportunity to be born again, to have a fresh start. He didn't stop acting creatively – anyone who believes in Christ can be a new creation.

In addition, God promises a new heaven and a new earth. The Lord seated on his throne, declares: 'I am making everything new!' (Revelation 21:5). This new earth will be free from sin, sickness, suffering and death. It will be Eden restored.

How wonderful is God's continuing creation, and how amazing that he invites us to be part of it all with him. Alongside his cocreators – the Holy Spirit and his Son, our Saviour Jesus Christ – we are called to join in with what God is doing. What a privilege, and what an opportunity.

However we express it, we have a God-given creativity which enables us to change our lives and those of the people around us, improving and celebrating our environment with our voices, hands, minds and spirits, making something new, original, surprising and special.

Through art, music and stories, colour, sound and imagination, we can partner with God in revealing something of the truth, power and beauty of who he is.

We shouldn't underestimate what we can contribute to God's kingdom through our creativity and what God can do through us creatively. It isn't about our ability, but about our heart and how much we are in tune with our creator.

Heavenly Father, thank you for all that you are, all that you have done and all that you will do. Help me to use my creativity to draw closer to you and to help build your kingdom. Amen.

CATHERINE LARNER

Jeremiah: the troubled prophet

Sara Batts-Neale writes…

Jeremiah is a hefty book of poetic oracle and prose narrative. It has a complicated political background with political powers waxing and waning. Jeremiah can be a tricky book to tackle, so we'll be looking at this in two parts. This week, we'll be thinking about Jeremiah as a person and what we can learn from him as a prophet. Later, towards the end of March, we'll be reflecting on the prophecies he gave.

While we remember that all scripture is God-inspired, we know that the texts weren't necessarily all written as contemporary accounts. It's understood that Jeremiah was edited and revised after the final exile. The writers were developing their theology after the events, attempting to explain the disasters that had befallen Judah at the hand of the neighbouring empires. Why did God let the disaster happen and how do we live now? What does it mean to be a prophet? What will the promised restoration of God's favour look like?

Some people have described passages in Jeremiah as like reading a personal diary, particularly those labelled as 'Confessions'. Others have said that the book appears to describe the role of an idealised prophet rather than a real person. I think the truth lies somewhere in between – there was a figure called Jeremiah, but not everything that is written happened exactly as described. Historically, writers would add ideas and details to make sure their readers knew what kind of prophet Jeremiah was. So, we'll need to bear that in mind as we work our way through ideas about the person of Jeremiah. We'll be talking about personality and character attributes even if they're not applying to one, single, verifiable historical figure. That's not to say there's not truth in these scriptures!

There is truth in Jeremiah's calls to the people to return to their covenant with God, and the spelling out of the disaster that will befall Jerusalem if his warning is not heeded. No one listens to him, and we see Jeremiah isolated, persecuted and frustrated. Jeremiah is sometimes called the 'Weeping Prophet' because of the depths of emotion we see. In the week to come we'll explore these challenges and emotions for the figure of Jeremiah – and how we can relate to them for our lives and our times, secure in the knowledge of God.

Record-breaking prophet

The word of the Lord came to him in the thirteenth year of the reign of Josiah son of Amon king of Judah. (v. 2, NIV)

What does it take to be a record breaker? Some of us will have an answer that springs from memories of childhood television: 'Dedication!'

King Josiah, the reforming king (you can read about him in 2 Kings 23), came to the throne aged 21 in 640BC. So that means Jeremiah's call happened in about 627BC. He is said to have continued to prophesy until 586BC, a 40-year role, making him the longest-serving prophet. He prophesied under three kings, trying to recall his hearers to the word of God as their world changed around them.

Jeremiah was dedicated – in both senses of the word. He was dedicated because he was tenacious, and he was dedicated because he was chosen by God. God had appointed him as a prophet from his birth. I wonder what it must have been like to work tirelessly and without reward for so long. It's increasingly rare to spend our paid working lives in one employment – in our working life, we generally have a choice of employer.

The opening verses of chapter 1 make it clear that Jeremiah, like other prophets before him, was called whether he wanted to be or not. Jeremiah's first reaction – that he wasn't old enough – is given short shrift by God. This example of a calling from birth is a blueprint for the idea of life-long vocation – a path in life we almost have no choice but to follow. Not everyone's work life looks like this though, and if ours does not, that doesn't make us less of a Christian or less valued in God's eyes. However, what Jeremiah does is set an example to follow, that regardless of our employment, listening to and sharing the word of God is in itself our lifetime's work.

'You did not choose me, but I chose you and appointed you so that you might go and bear fruit – fruit that will last – and so that whatever you ask in my name the Father will give you' (John 15:16).

SARA BATTS-NEALE

Fortified prophet

'They will fight against you but will not overcome you, for I am with you and will rescue you,' declares the Lord. (v. 19, NIV)

It's a bold claim, but I shall be banishing the idea of imposter syndrome from our lives today. Research shows that women will pass up a job opportunity if we don't match the requirements perfectly – but men will apply if they fit 60% of the job description. We just don't think we can do the job properly if we're not perfectly qualified. The good news is that when God calls us to something he will equip us.

Our calling might not be as a prophet of judgement, as Jeremiah was. As we will see during the rest of the week, we'll probably be very glad of that. It is not an easy life. Yet we will all, undoubtedly, be challenged in life to speak up and speak out, and to stand up for our faith and our choices at times. We may be called to difficult things and tricky places.

Yesterday Jeremiah claimed he wasn't old enough to speak. Today we read how God gave him the words to speak. We read too, that God promises that Jeremiah will have the strength he needs for the lifetime's work ahead. He may be reluctant – but he will be equipped. I love the idea of fortifications. God will build us up to be able to withstand the pressure, to create a space or to hold a boundary. The things we need, he will supply.

The life of a prophet and the life of a faithful Christian have two things in common – we do not have to be perfect to begin, and we can trust that God will equip us. You will be able to do the work that God has for you. You are not an imposter.

Where might you need reinforcements or new skills? Trust God today to show you how to find the opportunities to help you grow in faith.

SARA BATTS-NEALE

Realistic prophet

'So you shall speak all these words to them, but they will not listen to you. You shall call to them, but they will not answer you.' (v. 27, NRSV)

Have you ever had to deliver bad news to someone? It's heartbreaking, knowing we are turning someone's life upside down with news of a death or diagnosis, job loss or relationship breakdown. However, stating the facts clearly, even when they're uncomfortable, is the kindest thing we can do.

In today's reading, Jeremiah stands in the temple and proclaims judgement on the people of Judah. His news is not good for the people who have been living with the false belief that as long as God resides in the temple, no harm will come to it or them. The people are optimists with their hopes founded on the deception that their history is more important than their present actions. To them, Jeremiah sounds like a pessimist. Why shouldn't they continue making offerings to other gods, acting unjustly and oppressing the marginalised? They trust in the temple.

How frustrating it must have been to be sharing this message and to be ignored. Indeed, Jeremiah's words provoked the people against him, as we shall see at the end of March. Over and over again, Jeremiah brings the simple message: listen to God, walk in his ways and all will be well. Over and over again, the message is ignored. His message is unheeded – and it couldn't be clearer.

When we deliver bad news, there is the gut-wrenching moment when we see the recipient's comprehension and know we have been understood. There is nothing like that for Jeremiah. His prophetic life is one marked by incomprehension and rejection by the people of God. The coming of Jesus is the thing that will change the relationship, and we are called forward to that today as we remember Jesus' words in the temple. Jeremiah had real, bad news to bring – and we have real good news to share.

'It is written,' [Jesus] said to them, '"My house will be called a house of prayer," but you are making it "a den of robbers"' (Matthew 21:13, NIV).

SARA BATTS-NEALE

Questioning prophet

You are always righteous, Lord, when I bring a case before you. Yet I would speak with you about your justice: why does the way of the wicked prosper? (v. 1, NIV)

I once challenged a dog walker whose beautiful spaniel's failure to return when called made my dog nervous. The owner was indignant, calling me 'argumentative'. Little did he know I would take that as a badge of honour, not an insult! I have no fear of asking questions or disagreement. I'm also not worried about questioning God, and I value the gift of argument God gave me.

Jeremiah argues with God. I suspect many of us will have asked a version of the question he raises today, too. If, God, you're in control, then why do the treacherous thrive? Why doesn't truth, honesty, love and justice prevail? Everywhere we look, it seems that those who prosper are those who run after money, lie, exploit others and worship idols. Jeremiah wants to know why.

In the Old Testament there are many examples of questions posed to God – from Job, for example (Job 7:20), and Moses (Exodus 4:1). God takes those questions seriously. We see him answer Jeremiah today, even if there is not a lot of comfort for Jeremiah in the reply. God warns Jeremiah of treachery from those closest to him, reiterating coming disaster. That shepherds – who should be guiding and nurturing – have instead been agents of destruction, points to the false prophets and teachers leading the people astray with false hope. There is true hope in God's reply, but the lessons of faithfulness to God will need to be learned all over again.

Jeremiah's questioning shows us that God is very real to those who question him. In fact, I suspect it's probably worse to not question God – are we indifferent to the difficult questions? And if we seek resolutions to our troublesome questions, are we ready for the tough answers they contain?

'The God who made earth, made it liveable and lasting, known everywhere as God: "Call to me and I will answer you. I'll tell you marvellous and wondrous things that you could never figure out on your own"' (Jeremiah 33:2–3, MSG).

SARA BATTS-NEALE

Disappointed prophet

Why is my pain unceasing, my wound incurable, refusing to be healed? Truly, you are to me like a deceitful brook, like waters that fail.
(v. 18, NRSV)

For me, disappointment is one of the hardest feelings to sit with. It speaks of hopes dashed and expectations unfulfilled. I've found myself refusing to look forward to nice things in life for fear of the crashing disappointment that might be my lot. I know other people find great pleasure in anticipation and I often wish I could, but past disappointments hold greater sway for me than memories of when things went well.

I'm not sure Jeremiah ever had great hopes for his ministry. From the beginning God told him it would be difficult. We don't know quite how long Jeremiah had been prophesying when this conversation with God takes place, but he's been at it long enough to be disappointed.

Jeremiah had God's word as the delight of his heart. He did what was asked of him – sitting alone, away from merriment – but he's still being persecuted, and he is disappointed in God. He calls God a deceitful brook and a failing source of water. One can imagine the disappointment in a desert land of finding what looks like a life-giving spring only to find it is a short-lived stream. It is a powerful image to describe the sense of disillusionment and frustration Jeremiah is feeling.

Notice that God doesn't respond to that particular criticism. Instead, God promises again that he is with Jeremiah. He reiterates the idea of Jeremiah as a bronze wall, over whom the people will not prevail. We don't get to read Jeremiah's response, but I think today's reading shows us that even those closest to God don't always have beautiful words of praise. This gives us a powerful understanding that we can bring all our feelings to God – he's there and listening on the days we feel sad, lonely, woeful and disappointed.

'The Lord is near to the brokenhearted and saves the crushed in spirit' (Psalm 34:18).

SARA BATTS-NEALE

Lonely prophet

The word of the Lord came to me: 'You shall not take a wife, nor shall you have sons or daughters in this place.' (v. 1, NRSV)

I lived on my own for almost 15 years until I married Tim. Life alone was really hard at first, because it wasn't from choice, but eventually I revelled in it. When I moved to residential theological college it was a shock to be around people all the time. Yet they were also some of the loneliest moments when I wasn't part of the chatter or fun happening around me.

Loneliness is something Jeremiah had to deal with. His wasn't circumstantial, though, something to be overcome with a phone call or knocking on a neighbour's door. His was part and parcel of his calling as a prophet. God intended him to live his life of ministry alone. God commands him not to marry. More than that, Jeremiah is told to remove himself from all the rites of passage and celebrations around him. He is not to mourn the dead and must avoid the sounds of happiness.

It's not simply because God wants Jeremiah to be set apart. God tells Jeremiah that in the future, there won't be the community around to help mourners. The coming disaster will see to that. There will be no more happiness. Jeremiah, isolated, must live with this prophecy. I wonder if the burden of that knowledge would make it even harder to be part of celebrations, as those around him continue to ignore his warnings. There is exile to come, and the community will need to learn to live again.

Yet for all the prophecies which sound so difficult to our ears, the passage contains a promise of restoration – that God will regather his people from the lands to which they have been scattered. For now, though, Jeremiah must live and work alone in the isolated life of the prophet.

Lord God, we thank you that you lead your people in truth. Give us ready ears to listen to those who would shape our lives in response to your call on us to love you. Amen.

SARA BATTS-NEALE

Persecuted prophet

'Denounce him! Let us denounce him!' All my close friends are watching for me to stumble. (v. 10, NRSV)

Despite yesterday's optimistic note, there's not much in the book of Jeremiah that would qualify as a cheerful read. Today's verses most definitely wouldn't! We read of persecution and harassment – mocking voices greet his pronouncements and he is a laughingstock. It takes a strong person to be able to continue in the face of this kind of derision – and we recall now why on Monday we learned that God would give Jeremiah the protection he needed.

Several passages in the book of Jeremiah show us his inner turmoil and they have been labelled 'Confessions'. Our passage today is one example, and our reading on Thursday was another. They're also called laments (some have subsequently assumed that Jeremiah was also the writer of the book of Lamentations).

Lamenting is something we don't often make time for in our church or spiritual life, but it can be incredibly helpful. Jeremiah is clearly very fed up. He is persecuted by his close friends, and he is mocked by everyone. Yet he cannot stop – staying quiet is as physically and psychologically painful as continuing to speak. He feels overpowered by the need to speak out what his vocation has laid upon him. He is also miserable. Verses 7–10 are a catalogue of the reasons he's unhappy, and he brings them directly to God. Verses 14–18 are a wretched list of regrets that Jeremiah had ever been born, but even in the midst of this, Jeremiah praises God. In the middle of the catalogue of desolation and loneliness, Jeremiah remembers that God is on his side. 'The Lord is with me', he says (v. 11); 'Sing to the Lord; praise the Lord' (v. 13). He is also able to give the judgement of his persecutors over to God. That's the value in lamenting. Just as we reflected on Wednesday how questioning God can help us, so can bringing our woe to him. For in the process of spelling it out, we are reminded that the God we bring the woe to is the God who created us and loves us, and so we praise him.

Heavenly Father, I don't always come to prayer with joy and praise in my heart. Yet I know you listen to my soul in its sadness, and in the assurance of your closeness I find words to worship you. Amen.

SARA BATTS-NEALE

Saul: his fears and his fall

Tanya Marlow writes…

Studying Saul's life is a little like watching the 'Star Wars' prequels. If we have watched the original 'Star Wars' movies, we know that Anakin Skywalker eventually becomes Darth Vader, the formidable villain working for the Empire. But in the prequels, we root for Anakin and see all his potential as a great leader and the one to balance the Force. The pressure on him is so great, and we feel for him. But all the while we watch, we know his future, and that makes for painful viewing.

In our keenness to get to David's heroics, we perhaps skip over Saul's story, but as I've prepared these studies, I don't think I've ever been so emotionally attached to a Bible character. Like most real people, Saul is a complex, contradictory person who is at once so understandable and yet absolutely infuriating. If all you know about Saul is that he was the weak precursor to David, be prepared to meet him afresh.

What struck me most about Saul was that every decision he made had a powerful underlying emotion behind it, usually fear. He's fearful of the responsibility of being the first king, so he hides. Then he's fearful of not getting things right spiritually before battle, so he offers sacrifices instead of waiting for Samuel. Later, he's fearful of David's power and popularity, which turns into murderous jealousy. Above all, he's fearful of God, and not in the good way. As a result, he tries to placate God to get military success, as though the Lord is like a capricious pagan god to be appeased or manipulated. Saul's anger is initially holy, full of zeal for God's glory, then sours into a selfish, petty anger when he's not getting the glory.

Saul challenges us to look deeply at our emotions and to examine whether they're leading us away from God. Paul urged, 'In your anger do not sin' (Ephesians 4:26, NIV). A good summary for Saul might be: 'In your anxieties, do not sin.' As we journey through Saul's life, ask yourself: 'How are my emotions governing my actions?' Then take a leaf from David's book and set aside some time to pour out your emotions to the God who knows us and loves us.

Wandering into a calling

'About this time tomorrow I will send you a man from the land of Benjamin. Anoint him ruler over my people Israel; he will deliver them from the hand of the Philistines.' (v. 16, NIV)

When I was 22, I landed my dream job as a student minister. Overnight, I had a new calling. Having withered as an administrator, I couldn't wait to start. A decade later, I was enjoying life, leading and lecturing on a biblical theology programme, when overnight I became so disabled that I was virtually bedbound. It took a long time to rebuild from that point, and today I still need to spend 22 hours a day in bed. However, gradually I found a new calling as a writer.

Can you point to a similar day when your life was changed permanently, for better or worse? Maybe it was a diagnosis or the news of a death. Maybe it was a dream opportunity or a deep conviction to change.

For Saul, in the space of one day he lost his donkeys and found a crown. Only God was expecting that to happen. This was in the time of the judges when Samuel was leading Israel. The nation had never had a king before – there was no precedent for this. Even Samuel only had the barest of warnings himself that Saul would be king. This would change Samuel's calling, too, from judge to prophet. Neither Samuel nor Saul got any choice over it. It's something that happened to them rather than something they sought.

When our lives derail unexpectedly, even if it brings wonderful opportunities, it can be a shock and take a while to process. It can be helpful to realise that change in our lives inherently means we have a new calling. That was the old life, and there is no going back. This is the new. However we feel about our new life, there will be gifts from God within it, and the Lord will be leading us.

Think of a time when your life changed direction unexpectedly. Where was God at work in it? Pray over any situations of uncertainty or change: how is God calling you? What might you need to grieve?

TANYA MARLOW

God changed me (well, almost)

'The Spirit of the Lord will come powerfully upon you, and you will prophesy with them; and you will be changed into a different person.' (v. 6, NIV)

As a child, I was painfully shy. Today, I'm much more confident. When meeting a bunch of strangers, I barely get to counting to 'two-Mississippi' before words come tumbling, unbidden, out of my mouth. Before, I held my tongue; now, I hold forth.

Just occasionally, there's a situation that intimidates me so much that I revert into my childhood mind – terrified and silent. Afterwards I want to kick myself: 'Haven't I changed? Don't I know my own worth as God's child?' Perhaps you also have situations that send you screaming back to childhood or ways you thought you'd left behind. It's disheartening, but Saul's curious tale of being announced as king can encourage us.

Samuel predicts three events as a sign that God's hand would be with Saul, culminating in an outpouring of God's Spirit as Saul publicly prophesies. Saul's even told that he will 'be changed into a different person' (v. 6), which is surely a prayer most of us have uttered at some point.

Yet in the next verses, Saul's boldness disappears. When the lots are drawn, a way of showing the people of Israel that Saul as king is genuinely God's choice, not Samuel's, they have to hunt for Saul because he has 'hidden himself among the supplies' (v. 22). Despite his handsome, athletic appearance and coming from a well-respected family rich enough to own donkeys, Saul lacked confidence, even with God's Spirit.

Whenever we're called to a new venture, we can hold this paradox. Though our old self may peek through, God always, always equips those who are called. 2 Corinthians 3:18 promises that we 'are being transformed into his image with ever-increasing glory, which comes from the Lord, who is the Spirit'. The Spirit of Jesus in us really does change us, however slow it may feel.

Dear Lord, thank you that you renew me daily and are transforming me by your Holy Spirit. Where destructive old patterns of thinking or acting are coming through, please empower me to change. Amen.

TANYA MARLOW

When anger is positive

When Saul heard their words, the Spirit of God came powerfully upon him, and he burned with anger. (v. 6, NIV)

This chapter is Saul at his absolute best. Despite becoming king, his daily life as a farmer is humble. The story initially feels like the familiar pattern of the judges: an enemy threatens Israel, the people cry out, so God raises up a champion to save them. Saul is smart. He unites all the tribes into mass conscription through the use of threats – not against their lives, but their livelihoods; anyone who did not 'follow Saul and Samuel' (v. 7) would have their oxen killed. By naming himself alongside Samuel, Saul is uniting the old and new rulers, king and prophet together. He is a successful warrior-king and wins over the support of the whole nation. This is a new day for Israel and a very good one for Saul.

Though we know that Saul will later falter, it's important to remind ourselves that bad leaders often start out as great ones. It's a warning for us not to get complacent about our own morality, and it helps us remember that people are complex and villains don't announce themselves as bad from the get-go.

Above all, this passage shows us the power of God-given anger (v. 6). We tend to think of anger as something to avoid because of its damaging effects and loss of control, but we can forget that anger can be positive. Anger is the natural, holy response to injustice. Whenever we're feeling powerless at the state of the world or a more personal issue of injustice, we can turn to our anger, which gives us the energy and courage to act, gather others together and seek God's strength to right wrongs, even battling to do so. Today, think through areas of injustice where you feel powerless, and ask for God-given anger that leads to action.

Dear Lord Jesus, who drove out temple traders with whips and overturned tables for the sake of justice, please give me the kind of anger at injustice that leads to action and righteousness. Amen.

TANYA MARLOW

When disobedience looks like piety

'You have done a foolish thing,' Samuel said. 'You have not kept the command the Lord your God gave you; if you had, he would have established your kingdom over Israel for all time.' (v. 13, NIV)

Sometimes a good thing can be a bad thing because the wrong person is doing it. For example, my son made me a lovely cake but got into trouble because he was eight and not allowed to use the oven unsupervised.

Saul was baffled by Samuel's rebuke and trotted out his justifications for offering pre-battle sacrifices. His entire calling as king was to defeat the Philistines (1 Samuel 9:16), and he felt the pressure. His son Jonathan had just rashly provoked the enemy. The Philistines had gathered a vast army (v. 5). Plus, he waited seven days for Samuel (though, crucially, not to the end of the day), his men were fleeing and he wanted God's favour (vv. 11–12). He was doing all the right, strategic, pious things. It's all so understandable.

However, we have a few clues in earlier verses as to why what Saul did was wrong. Samuel had a unique role at this time as God's mouthpiece: 'If someone went to enquire of God, they would say, "Come, let us go to the seer"' (1 Samuel 9:9), and the people had to wait for Samuel before eating because 'he must bless the sacrifice' (1 Samuel 9:13). So, Samuel's instruction to Saul to wait seven days for Samuel to offer the sacrifice and issue further orders (1 Samuel 10:8) should be seen as God's command, and Saul broke it. As a result, Saul's kingship would not become a dynasty; his son would not succeed him.

God always prefers obedience to religious observance. It's a tough question to ask ourselves: where are we simply box-ticking in our walk with God, and where are we truly seeking to obey him? Even kings must listen to the prophets of the day. What do we need to hear?

King of heaven, we are sorry when the pressures of life cause us to jump the gun and act without first praying and seeking your will. Please forgive us when we ignore your word out of fear that it's impossible. Amen.

TANYA MARLOW

Making unnecessary rules

Saul had bound the people under an oath, saying, 'Cursed be anyone who eats food before evening comes, before I have avenged myself on my enemies!'… Jonathan said, 'My father has made trouble for the country.' (vv. 24, 29, NIV)

Whether it's with church, work or caring responsibilities, whenever there's pressure on us to achieve, it can lead to anxiety. We then try to control the outcome with arbitrary rules or unachievable targets. I see this in the boundaries I set for my son: behaviours I'm normally relaxed about suddenly become unacceptable when he's with 'company'. I fear the judgement of others, and I pass that fear on to him in the form of rules.

This is exactly what Saul did. He was so desperate to defeat the Philistines that he told his army not to eat until they had won the battle: stick, not carrot. As incentives go, it's entirely ineffectual because they're weaker for battle as a result (vv. 28–30). Jonathan, who didn't know about the oath and ate honey, is there to tell us that this rule is ridiculous. Ironically, the men were so ravenous at the end of the day that they gorged themselves on meat, not waiting to drain the blood out before cooking it (vv. 31–34). In keeping Saul's rule, they ended up breaking God's law.

When God goes silent on Saul before battle, he assumes it's because of someone's sin. Like Jephthah before him (Judges 11:29–40), he makes a foolish vow to kill even his son, and the lot falls on Jonathan. What did God want in all this? Saul interprets the lots as God's will to make good on his vow, but it makes more sense to agree with the army that God wanted the truth to come out but spare Jonathan (vv. 44–46). The problem wasn't Jonathan's rule-breaking but Saul's rules.

Jesus later condemned the Pharisees for adding superfluous commandments to God's law (Matthew 23:1–4), but it's tempting to do it today whenever we feel like we're losing control. Let's ditch those unnecessary, burdensome expectations.

Ask yourself: what rules or expectations have I put on myself that have not come from God? In what areas of my life am I being too harsh on others? Pray for God's guidance and clarity.

TANYA MARLOW

No pick 'n' mix religion

'For… arrogance [is] like the evil of idolatry. Because you have rejected the word of the Lord, he has rejected you as king.' (v. 23, NIV)

If you've never heard this passage preached before, I can tell you why in one word: genocide. It's very difficult to get beyond God's shocking command to kill an entire nation, including women and children (v. 3).

Though it remains problematic, I find some things helpful. First, nothing in this passage justifies genocide today: Jesus' teaching to turn the other cheek (Matthew 5:39) means Christians are to be peacemakers (Matthew 5:9). Second, I consider God's judgement on Egypt: Pharaoh killed a generation of Hebrew babies, so God's angel later killed the Egyptian's firstborn during the Passover. Though it's still brutal, there's justice there. God had previously warned that the Amalekites were marked for judgement because they had attacked the Israelites when they were at their most vulnerable (Deuteronomy 25:17–19) and King Agag was personally responsible for killing many Israelite children (v. 33). Third, despite Samuel's best efforts, the Amalekites seem to survive in some way and are still there to make trouble for David later (1 Samuel 30:1–20).

Even if we're still troubled by God's command, there's nothing to excuse Saul's behaviour. This isn't a normal war, but a solemn obligation to bring God's judgement. Saul kills the people but spares the murderous king and the best loot (v. 9). He obeys only the parts of God's commands that suit him, then promptly builds a monument to his own glory (v. 12). After Saul's former anxiety to get things right, there's a new arrogance here.

Samuel grieves deeply for a night, wrestling with God for his former protégé before delivering the devastating judgement: God had rejected Saul as king (v. 23). This is a warning to us: where in our lives do we pick and choose God's commands, then build a monument in our honour?

If yesterday's admonition was to avoid adding to God's law, today's is avoiding taking away from God's law. Which of God's commands do you find daunting or impossible? Ask the Spirit to help you in your weakness.

TANYA MARLOW

Our unexpected healer

Whenever the spirit from God came on Saul, David would take up his lyre and play. Then relief would come to Saul. (v. 23, NIV)

As someone who's had recurrent clinical depression over the years, I know the harm it can cause when Christians label an illness as either a personal defect or affliction by demons. Additionally, because through Jesus, Christians have the Holy Spirit living within them permanently (e.g. 1 Corinthians 6:19), it's vital that we know that Saul's supernaturally caused mental distress, whatever it was, is not transferable to Christians today.

After Saul's sin, the blessing and presence of the Holy Spirit leaves Saul and comes upon David. In its place, a bad, or harmful, spirit 'from God' terrifies Saul (vv. 14–15). We shouldn't understand this as God sending a demon. In the thought-world of the Hebrew Bible, everything that happens, even disaster, is automatically seen as coming from God's hand. There may be an element of supernatural, active punishment for Saul's disobedience. Alternatively, these attacks may be somehow a natural consequence of God's Spirit leaving him, or of Saul's growing paranoia as he knows God has rejected him as king.

The main point is that David is the only one who can help Saul. Here, David served him so well he was promoted to armour-bearer. The text translated 'Saul liked him very much' could equally be translated 'Saul loved David greatly', and either way, there was no animosity (v. 21). It's as if God is whispering a message to Saul through this relationship: David is not the enemy; he will bring healing.

It can be hard to accept help or service from others, especially if we're proud, but sometimes that's how God works. Healing often comes from unexpected quarters, and we need to be alert to the whispers of God. For those of us with mental illness, relief may come through any combination of therapy, pills and prayer, all gifts of God.

Lord, we thank you that your Holy Spirit is with us and will not depart from us. Please draw us to people and places of healing. Please bring relief to all those tormented by mental illness today. Amen.

TANYA MARLOW

Going all in with God

'The Lord who rescued me from the paw of the lion and the paw of the bear will rescue me from the hand of this Philistine.' Saul said to David, 'Go, and the Lord be with you.' (v. 37, NIV)

Though I'd never condone gambling, our family sometimes plays poker with plastic chips. I'm a good poker player, but not a great one, because I lack the confidence to go all in, unblinking, when there's a really good hand. I want to hold something back in case it all goes wrong.

Here the stakes are high: one man-to-man battle to decide whether the Philistines or the Israelites win the war. It needs to be the right fighter. Saul has learnt his lesson after the disaster of threatening his troops with hunger (1 Samuel 14:24) and now offers bribery instead: his daughter's hand in marriage and wealth (v. 25). David jumps at the chance, motivated perhaps partly by the reward, but mainly because he's outraged at the offence to 'the living God' (v. 26). To Saul's great credit, when this deeply unsuitable volunteer comes forward (v. 33), he stakes Israel's entire future on a shepherd boy because he sees David's faith (v. 37). His cautious streak comes through again when he gives David his armour (v. 38), but David knows in a way Saul never has that his hope of victory rests in God's power alone and he goes boldly ahead unshielded (v. 39). Saul shows that he is a good poker player when it comes to the things of God, but David is a great one.

It is never a mistake to go 'all in' with God. Maybe that means worshipping God wholeheartedly, leaving nothing behind and expending yourself in praise. Maybe that means stretching your trust muscles in uncertain times, leaning on the God who can do 'immeasurably more than all we ask or imagine' (Ephesians 3:20). Maybe it means jumping on a crazy opportunity because you recognise the Spirit's nudge. Whatever else happens in life, trusting God is our best bet.

Think through the different areas of your life and your relationship with God. Where are you holding back from God? What things are you keeping out of God's reach?

TANYA MARLOW

Becoming a mirror

Saul was very angry; this refrain displeased him greatly. 'They have credited David with tens of thousands,' he thought, 'but me with only thousands. What more can he get but the kingdom?' (v. 8, NIV)

What makes a good leader? Anne, a business consultant, once told me that a good leader should be a window when it comes to criticism and a mirror when it comes to success. In other words, the leader should accept criticism of the organisation personally, as they're ultimately responsible, but let their team take the credit for victories and shine the glory on them.

If this is true, then Saul is a very bad leader. David had just won a major battle for him, and now he was highly successful in the army. This means more Philistines killed and, if we remember, God's commission to Saul when he became king was defeating the Philistines (1 Samuel 9:16). With David's help, they're winning against the Philistines (v. 5) and the people celebrate both Saul and David (v. 7). There is no bad news here. With David in his team, Saul is succeeding in his mission, but he can only see the negative: he wants the whole credit and he wants all the glory.

The key point to note for the rest of Saul's journey into murderous madness is that all this was not inevitable. Sure, he would lose the kingdom, but he didn't have to give in to anger and jealousy. Jonathan's reaction is to symbolically hand over the garments of his future kingship to David – willingly, gladly, lovingly (vv. 3–4). If only Saul had done this, so much needless suffering would have been avoided.

Who do you get jealous of or feel irritated by? When do you feel like you need all the glory? Can you pinpoint why? Sometimes what feels like losing is actually a win-win. If there's someone you currently resent for their success or well-being, challenge yourself to spend some time praying blessing over them.

Dear God, please may we be like Jesus, who didn't grasp at glory but 'humbled himself by becoming obedient to death – even death on a cross!' (Philippians 2:8). Forgive our jealousy and help us to rest in you. Amen.

TANYA MARLOW

Fear versus love

Saul was afraid of David, because the Lord was with David but had departed from Saul… When Saul saw how successful he was, he was afraid of him. (vv. 12, 15, NIV)

I have been mainly bedbound with severe chronic illness for more than a decade. It's hard. Recently, I heard that someone else with chronic illness had recovered. Usually, my instinct is to rejoice over others' healing, but this time I was surprised: my gut reaction was anger. When I dug deeper, I realised that beneath the anger lay fear – fear that she would now leave our friendship behind, fear that she would see me as negative and part of her past.

So, before we condemn Saul for his self-defeating violent rage, let's remember that beneath his anger was fear, and fear is a powerful driver. Here, Saul tries to kill David three times. Shockingly, the first is during a time of prophesying, which is perhaps why the writer attributes Saul's anger to an evil spirit (v. 10), for surely he could not have done something so blasphemous by himself. Then Saul sends David away to war (v. 13). Finally, he fulfils his former promise to give David his daughter's hand in marriage, 'so that she may be a snare to him' (v. 21), and he sets the bride price at 100 Philistine foreskins, 'for David to fall by the hands of the Philistines' (v. 25). Why? Despite being the one with a spear, Saul was afraid because he had lost God's presence to David (v. 12), because David was successful (v. 15) and because David was beloved (vv. 16, 28).

Consider: are you currently jealous of someone's success, popularity or even their relationship with God? How should we respond? I come back to the Bible's promise: 'Perfect love drives out fear' (1 John 4:18). We receive God's perfect love so we can truly love others. Today, we return to that truth: we are deeply, deeply loved by God.

Where do you feel twinges of jealousy? What fear lies beneath? Spend some time meditating today on Romans 8:35–39 and 1 John 4:16–19.

TANYA MARLOW

Stop early in your sin

That day [Doeg] killed eighty-five men who wore the linen ephod. He also put to the sword Nob, the town of the priests, with its men and women, its children and infants, and its cattle, donkeys and sheep. (vv. 18–19, NIV)

By this stage in the story, we might still have some sympathy for Saul. He starts out so shyly and seems desperate to prove himself as king, clumsily trying to follow God's orders one minute, making excuses for foolish behaviour the next, stumbling and slipping, with occasional flashes of goodness. Even his alarming violence towards David comes from a place we can relate to – common jealousy and insecurity. But once we get to this scene, it is hard even for a sympathetic audience to find him redeemable.

Whether Ahimelek truly believed David's lie that he was on a secret mission from Saul, or whether he guessed at the reason David needed bread and let him have Goliath's sword to defend himself, his 'crime' was disproportionately, shockingly punished. Even Saul's guards knew that killing priests was a step too far and they refused the king's command.

Let's pause the scene there. The guards are Saul's conscience. Even in the midst of his anger, there's a choice. There's always a choice. Saul coldly destroyed a whole village and ordered the death of 85 priests.

There is always a moment, a decision point, when formerly good leaders step over the line and become evil, and sadly church leaders are not immune to this. We need this story to shock us. If you're flirting with sin or developing bad habits which you know to be wrong, stop. Stop now. Stop before one day you say to yourself, 'Oh, I don't care anymore, I'm just going to do it.' Stop before it wreaks destruction on others. Have people around you to be your 'second conscience', be honest and get help as soon as possible – because in Saul we can see where the train track ends, and it's not pretty.

Ask yourself: is there any path I'm starting to follow in my life that may end badly? Who are my 'second consciences'? Who might I need to be a 'second conscience' for, to protect them from sinning?

TANYA MARLOW

Fighting against God

'May the Lord reward you well for the way you treated me today.
I know that you will surely be king and that the kingdom of Israel will
be established in your hands.' (vv. 19–20, NIV)

'So, shall I say yes to this curacy in Plymouth?' my husband asked me. Jon
had been training for ministry in Oxford, and I had close friends and great
opportunities locally. Then I looked on a map and discovered that what
I thought was Plymouth was actually Portsmouth, and Plymouth was six
hours away from my parents. It felt like an easy no, but it wouldn't go away.
The position was an excellent fit for Jon, and I knew the pull of the Holy
Spirit was directing us there. I argued with God for a while, then gave in,
with some trepidation. While in Plymouth, I became disabled, and it was
by far the best place for that to have happened. God had provided for us.

Saul had become so obsessed with chasing down David that he was
neglecting fighting the Philistines (v. 1). When David showed him mercy,
Saul 'wept aloud' (v. 16). No reassurances that David was not a threat were
anywhere near as powerful as witnessing the person Saul had labelled as
an enemy behaving like a friend. His statement is extraordinary: 'I know
that you will surely be king' (v. 20). This shows that Saul really did know
that God planned for David to have the throne, and that David deserved it.
In going against David, Saul had been going against God – and he knew it.

Maybe you can feel the nudges of the Spirit pulling you away from an
area or role that you've loved. Maybe you need to give up a grudge against
someone, however entitled you are to feel angry at them. Saul's story
reminds us that there is nothing more futile than fighting against God.
When we give in to God, it can feel like loss, but it's always gain.

---

*Dear Lord, I don't want to fight you. May your Holy Spirit lead me to know
your will in the big plans I'm making and the everyday battles I face. Please
guide me today. Amen.*

TANYA MARLOW

A disastrous legacy

But David thought to himself, 'One of these days I shall be destroyed by the hand of Saul. The best thing I can do is to escape to the land of the Philistines.' (27:1, NIV)

After Saul's moving realisation yesterday, we yearn for a happy ending. God had set it all up for him. Saul could have abdicated his leadership, as Samuel had done, and passed on the throne to David with Jonathan's blessing. Infuriatingly, incomprehensibly, Saul instead pursued David, and again Saul's life was spared. What we may miss in the repetition, however, is the consequences of Saul refusing to learn his lesson.

Forgiveness and grace are one thing, risking your life is quite another, and David needs to flee. As a direct result of Saul's actions, David left to live with the Philistines because even the enemies of God were less dangerous than his own king (27:1). He was away for over a year (27:7). This meant that Israel no longer had its champion warrior to fight the Philistines, which in turn meant that the Philistines had the upper hand and killed many, including Saul and – tragically – Jonathan (1 Samuel 31:1–3). Because David had disappeared from Israel at a crucial time, there was no easy transition of power. After Saul's death, civil war erupted, and 'The war between the house of Saul and the house of David lasted a long time' (2 Samuel 3:1). The consequences of Saul's repeated sin were far-reaching and disastrous.

Saul's experience shows us that when God teaches us something important, it's vital that we learn it and so avoid continuing in serious sin. My friend Amy Boucher Pye is a great advocate for spiritual journalling. When we take time to reflect on and record what God has taught us, we can remember essential lessons more easily and be spared the consequences of carrying on in our destruction.

If you have a spiritual journal, look through the past year. Spend time thanking God for the answers to prayer, the truths revealed and the changes in you. If you don't yet journal, why not start today?

TANYA MARLOW

Lamenting the unrepentant

[Saul] was afraid; terror filled his heart. He enquired of the Lord, but the Lord did not answer him by dreams or Urim or prophets. Saul then said to his attendants, 'Find me… a medium' (vv. 5–7, NIV)

Do you have anyone in your life who seems bent on self-sabotage, no matter how much help they get? It's very hard to witness. Having upheld the Lord's command to ban spirits and mediums, Saul's last act is to break God's law and try to manipulate God's will. He failed to realise that God's silence is sometimes a message in itself (v. 6). Saul's desperation for success makes him grasp for the good old days, only for a ghostly Samuel to reveal God's judgement as a death sentence (vv. 16–19). The king whom God appointed to rid the land of Philistines (1 Samuel 9:16) would be defeated by them. Saul, who started humbly with a true desire to please God and save the people, ended up destroying his dynasty, his legacy and his nation. It's heartbreaking and infuriating, in equal measure.

I feel that way about contemporary Christian leaders who have been publicly disgraced. It's horrifying to learn that ministers who started so well and were so obviously anointed by God ended up abusing others and refusing to acknowledge their wrongdoing. It can be confusing, too: how could God bless their ministry when they were secretly emotionally, sexually or physically abusive?

Saul's story helps answer this question. He had so many chances to do the right thing, but he continued, agonisingly, to make destructive choices. God delayed his judgement for a while, but ultimately passed the kingdom on to David who, despite his faults, wholeheartedly loved the Lord. What do we do when leaders break our hearts? Like David, we lament: 'How the mighty have fallen!' (2 Samuel 1:19). Before some leaders fall in death, they fall spiritually. We can grieve both events, finding comfort in God's justice and faithfulness.

Dear Lord, we bring you the Sauls in our lives: the self-saboteurs, the ones who refuse to change, the abusers, the leaders who let us down. Lord, in our lament, keep us humble. Comfort us, we pray. Amen.

TANYA MARLOW

Silence and solitude

Di Archer writes…

Welcome to the next few days of silence and solitude. Does the prospect of delving into these two topics appeal to or dismay you? Perhaps your circumstances are such that both silence and solitude are just pipe dreams? If so, I can relate – I am not sure if this is mainly about personality type, lifestyle or denominational experience, but it seems that friends of mine are far better than me at carving out time for both quiet and being alone. It just seems to come naturally to them.

Wherever you sit on the spectrum, I hope you enjoy the coming days of considering some of what the Bible says about silence and solitude. I have certainly found it fascinating to trace some common themes stretching through the centuries across both the Old and New Testaments. In contrast to the culture of today, which encourages us to take 'me time', the biblical focus is firmly on the opportunities of 'alone time' to engage with God. If you think that sounds rather a high calling, you will be reassured by the people we will encounter throughout our Bible studies.

In our age of unprecedented connection with others through media, music, podcasts, television and screens, where we are bombarded with information and incoming news, perhaps we need to rediscover the power of 'down time' with God. In a world that is busy trying to create virtual reality in many forms, do we need to be the rebels who learn how to deal well with actual reality? Could it be that those who embrace silence and solitude are the extremists here – giving us permission to rediscover the unmatchable joy of relationship with our creator God, restoring our perspective, giving us back truth in a world of spin doctors and fake news, and slowing us down for a moment, so that we can catch a breath of eternity to give meaning to our lives?

Join me as we take a walk on the wild side. Let's refuse to believe that being busy equals being important. Let's try, from our own unique starting point, to explore the delights of some silence and solitude with our loving heavenly Father.

Being silent – how to begin

Let us draw near to God with a sincere heart and with the full assurance that faith brings, having our hearts sprinkled to cleanse us from a guilty conscience and having our bodies washed with pure water. Let us hold unswervingly to the hope we profess, for he who promised is faithful. (vv. 22–23, NIV)

Depending on your Christian tradition, you have probably heard so many ideas about how to spend 'quiet time' with God. For me, they range from Susannah Wesley (the mother of hymn-writer Charles and Methodist-founder John), who famously flipped her apron over her head to get some peace from her children to pray, to amazing tales of Christians trekking up prayer mountains to engage with God. Whether you have established patterns of prayer or wrestle with guilt that you are not spending enough time with God, whether you find talking to God easier in your faith community or alone, this encouragement from the writer of Hebrews gives us our starting place.

Because Jesus has put us completely in the right with God, we can come near to God. For the Jews the writer was addressing, this meant that the purification rituals they adhered to were no longer necessary. Through Jesus' death and resurrection, they were now totally in the clear. As are we. We do not have to be afraid – neither of God's judgement nor of our self-condemnation. Jesus has opened the door and welcomes us into the Father's presence. Whenever, wherever, we are free to come, free to hope, free to trust in the goodness of God.

So how will you find your way over these next couple of weeks to explore silence and solitude for yourself? There are no rules. Why not try something new? If you usually chatter away to God on a walk, try to listen to him instead. If you're soothing the baby, sing a worship song. If you are on a bus, in a car, waiting in a queue, think about how you can use the time to draw near to the one who loves you completely.

Dear Father, please meet me as I turn my attention and my heart towards you. Thank you. Amen.

DI ARCHER

Enforced solitude

But while Joseph was there in the prison, the Lord was with him; he showed him kindness and granted him favour in the eyes of the prison warder. So the warder put Joseph in charge of all those held in the prison, and he was made responsible for all that was done there. (vv. 20–22, NIV)

As we dip into the lives of a few biblical characters, see which ones you relate to most. I have always been rather in awe of Joseph and his determination to trust God in the face of utterly undeserved hardship. Sure, he came from a dysfunctional blended family, was the spoilt favourite son and had severely upset his brothers with his dreams of grandeur (Genesis 37:1–7), but he did not deserve their violent rejection. All the pent-up resentment and jealousy boiled over one day in the desert, and they threw him down a well to rot. Only one brother's pity spared him – yet his ensuing slavery in Egypt still led him to another seemingly dead end: prison. Somehow, he clung to his faith and was rewarded for his integrity. Joseph's enforced solitude bore incredible fruit, leading step by step to the governing of Egypt, the rescue of his family and a vital part of our salvation history.

Few of us get through life without times of enforced limitations. Solitude can be imposed upon us through illness, tragedy, mental health issues and other unchosen circumstances. You may be in one of those times right now. It is hard to lean into the challenges and keep trusting in God's good purposes, even if we have known God's faithfulness to date. Yet what was true for Joseph – 'the Lord was with him' (v. 21) – is also true for us, and God is still kind. I try to remember to look for the signs of his grace, even when I am feeling desperately tossed and buffeted by the waves of difficulties. I often depend on my prayer partner to help me. If your solitude is feeling more like isolation, sometimes it is good to invite in a trusted friend.

Read Luke 7:11–17. Jesus is reliable in tough times of enforced solitude. He meets us where we are.

DI ARCHER

Solitude makes us shine

When Moses came down from Mount Sinai with the two tablets of
the covenant law in his hands, he was not aware that his face was
radiant because he had spoken with the Lord. When Aaron and all the
Israelites saw Moses, his face was radiant, and they were afraid to
come near him. (vv. 29–30, NIV)

We might regard Moses as being extraordinary and not really like us.
He grew up in a palace, killed a man in anger, ran away to the desert,
learnt shepherding, met the woman of his dreams and then encountered
a strange burning bush. Not many of us are invited to rescue a complete
nation, but it is notable that Moses' significant engagements with God were
mostly in solitude. From the bush (Exodus 3:1–4) to Mount Sinai (19:3),
from the tent of meeting to enquire of the Lord (33:7–11) to the establish-
ment of the law for the Israelites (20:21) and the receiving of the new stone
tablets (34:2–3), the Lord spoke to Moses when he was alone with him. How
remarkable that the time they spent together showed on his face.

I have seen something similar in some Christians. It's hard to put into
words, but there is just something about their presence that is different,
radiant even. They make me feel better, just by being around them. Is this
the potential of time spent alone with our amazing God – a luminosity,
brightness and warmth that draws us near to him, and then emanates out
to others, whether we realise it or not? How do we get close enough to God
for that to happen? I want it to happen – to take the time to allow God's
presence to soak into me such that I am warmed and strengthened. I think
it does take time, just like any other relationship. We need to spend quality
time with God if we want to reflect him to the world. While he walks with
us every day, who knows how much better that could be if we stop and
give him our attention.

---

*Moses had to go up a mountain to meet with God, but we are invited to step
boldly into his presence right where we are (read Hebrews 10:19–25).*

DI ARCHER

When God is silent

The Lord said to Job: 'Will the one who contends with the Almighty correct him? Let him who accuses God answer him!' Then Job answered the Lord: 'I am unworthy – how can I reply to you?… I spoke once, but I have no answer – twice, but I will say no more.' (vv. 1–5, NIV)

I have yet to meet a Christian who has not had a comparable experience to Job. Even if they have not lost family, possessions, livelihood, health and support from family and friends like Job did, they have known the 'dark night of the soul' (a phrase coined by John of the Cross in the 16th century). For reasons that invariably involve deeply difficult circumstances, the sense of God's presence vanishes, and the joy along with it. No amount of determination overcomes this horrible experience. Depression often stalks the sufferer.

I have been there. Have you? God seems silent. I have wrestled with what this might mean. Has God the Almighty forgotten me? Have I done something unforgivable? Why are things getting worse, not better? How can this be, and how do I bear the unbearable?

At these times, one of which was the long, dark tunnel of severe eating disorders hitting our family and frightening me out of my mind, I have leaned on others, depending on them to pray and trust for me. They knew that God's silence did not mean he had left the building. It did not mean he did not hear my cries. They encouraged me to keep talking to God, no matter what. I am grateful for friends who were and are so much more balanced than Job's.

In the end, God did have the last word with Job. He waited for Job to be honest with him, then generously refuted Job's complaints point by point (chapters 38—41). He answered Job in his own time and revealed his greatness and glory. Despite feeling abandoned for so long, Job discovered the riches in God's silence and was drawn into a deeper, more secure relationship with him.

Read Psalm 5. Being honest changed the psalmist's perspective. How might his words inspire your own prayers?

DI ARCHER

Hiding from God

The Lord turned to him and said, 'Go in the strength you have and save Israel out of Midian's hand. Am I not sending you?'… Gideon replied, 'But how can I save Israel? My clan is the weakest in Manasseh, and I am the least in my family.' (vv. 14–15, NIV)

It's a bit of a theme with those whom God calls. Despite encountering miraculous burning bushes or angels of the Lord appearing in person, there is still a reluctance to trust and obey. So the argument that we would believe if only we could hear the audible voice of God or see writing on the wall really isn't sustainable.

Our nervous hero Gideon was in inappropriate solitude, hiding in fear of the oppressing Midianites, threshing wheat in secret to save it from confiscation. In that difficult place of fear and secrecy, God came to meet with him. Not only did he appear in angelic form, but he also spoke words of prophetic truth over him, calling him a 'mighty warrior' (v. 12). The angel saw in Gideon what Gideon could not see in himself. In that place of solitude, God called out of him qualities that would develop to change his situation and that of his nation.

You could call it a bit of a risk of spending time in quiet and solitude with God. What if, like Gideon, he asks you to do something you don't feel ready for? What if his view of you challenges your view of yourself? What if he sees you as stronger than you feel? What if he asks you to let go of fears or to stop hiding? What if you have always felt unloved or second rate, and he says you are beloved and gifted? Will you, like Gideon, trust that God's promise to be with you (v. 16) is enough? It could be that even if you are protecting yourself in the quiet place of silence and solitude, God still meets with you there and speaks to you about a new adventure.

Gideon's first brave act was done under cover of darkness because he was still afraid (v. 27). God doesn't expect you to change overnight, but just to start the journey.

DI ARCHER

Rooted in God's word

Blessed is the one… whose delight is in the law of the Lord, and who meditates on his law day and night. That person is like a tree planted by streams of water, which yields its fruit in season and whose leaf does not wither – whatever they do prospers. (vv. 1–3, NIV)

Psalm 1 is one of my favourites. It makes it plain that there are two ways set before us. Will we choose God's way, or will we choose another path – which the unknown psalmist calls the 'way of sinners' – destined for misery? In contrast, the psalmist reassures us that choosing God's way brings blessing to ourselves and others. Make the choice again today!

The psalm also paints a powerful picture of what it means to be rooted in God's word. What does it mean to you to 'delight in the law of the Lord' and 'meditate' on it? There are no rules here as to how to meditate or whether we always need silence and solitude to do so, just the stark truth that whatever we put into our hearts and minds will be what comes out. This doesn't necessarily mean learning scripture off by heart or spending hours on our knees, although it might. It's more the principle. How do you fill yourself with God's truth and refute lies? How do you use quiet moments with God to savour his word and let it fill your thoughts?

There are so many ways of doing this! My friend annotates Bible verses and mounts them in beautiful frames; another scribbles them on sticky notes and puts them on her mirror. I find worship fixes the words in my mind. There are some great apps for daily devotions out there too. *Lectio divina* is a popular way of entering into Bible stories, or perhaps scouring commentaries brings scripture to life for you. What might you try this week?

Read John 7:37–38. Find your way to permeate your soul with God's word, and the promise is that you will be able to draw on a stream of life-giving water that never runs dry.

DI ARCHER

Unhappy solitude

Elijah was afraid and ran for his life… 'I have had enough, Lord,' he said. 'Take my life'… All at once an angel touched him and said, 'Get up and eat.' He looked around, and there by his head was some bread baked over hot coals, and a jar of water. (vv. 3–6, NIV)

This pivotal episode in Elijah's life is packed with incredible revelations about the nature of God. After Elijah's triumph on Mount Carmel (1 Kings 18:16–39), where he proved the faithfulness of Yahweh and slew hundreds of prophets of Baal, he was on the run from Queen Jezebel's death threats. From such a victory, Elijah plummeted to despair and fear, and he escaped with just one servant to the wilderness. His emotional high slid all the way to a suicidal depression. He collapsed under a broom tree and wanted to die, convinced that he was alone in his loyalty to the true God.

This adrenaline slump is a recognisable human reaction to great output and achievement. Elijah was spent. His solitude was not a happy place; he complained to God and then escaped into the exhausted silence of sleep.

God treated him so compassionately. He asked Elijah what was wrong and encouraged him to name his emotions. He didn't rebuke him for his skewed perspectives. He met his physical needs – restoring, resting, feeding and watering. God revealed his own nature in a whisper and reminded Elijah gently of the truth that he was not alone, but one of 7,000 God-followers. Then he took Elijah on the next steps into his future, giving him a trusted companion to work with. God gave Elijah incredible, personal and appropriate care.

We don't have to get times of silence and solitude 'right' in order to meet with God. We don't have to follow a formula or do it the same every time. We just have to be honest with our heavenly Father about how we are feeling and remember how good he is. God will meet us there because he really does care.

What question do you think God might be asking you today?

DI ARCHER

God's longing to restore

'In repentance and rest is your salvation, in quietness and trust is your strength, but you would have none of it'… Yet the Lord longs to be gracious to you; therefore he will rise up to show you compassion. For the Lord is a God of justice. Blessed are all who wait for him! (vv. 15, 18, NIV)

I confess that the opening verse here about repentance and rest is so familiar to me that I was surprised to find it nestled in this dramatic outburst by Isaiah on the oscillating fortunes of Israel. Isaiah is expressing, on God's behalf, the overwhelming desire that God has to gather, bless and heal his people in every way – yet also how painful is the reluctance of these very people to let him do that. The raw emotion tumbles through the words, conveying God's deepest longings to restore and rain down abundance on the people he loves. Here too is the reassurance that God will guide (v. 21), readily respond (v. 19) and reveal truth (v. 20). All that God asks for in return is that his people turn to him and trust him.

Like Israel, it is all too easy for us to go it alone and think we know best. Instead of dedicating ourselves to enjoying God's presence and quietening our restless souls, we dash about thinking we can solve our own problems – or is that just me? Like Israel, which was harassed by surrounding enemy nations, we too can try to find our own 'horses' (v. 16) to escape on. Yet we miss out on so much when we do! At their best, times of silence and solitude with God are opportunities to bring ourselves before him, in honesty and humility, humbly trusting him for the way ahead. We cannot save ourselves or deliver our own justice.

It's a recurring theme throughout the prophetic books of the Old Testament that people just don't realise how brilliant, how compassionate, how willing to bless, how absolutely good God our Father is. Isaiah begs God's people to discover these truths again. This isn't just theology – it is God's love for you.

Do you want salvation and strength? They are found in repentance, rest, quietness and trust. Find them today.

DI ARCHER

Solitude and joy

The angel said to him, 'I am Gabriel. I stand in the presence of God, and I have been sent to speak to you and to tell you this good news. And now you will be silent and not able to speak until the day this happens, because you did not believe my words, which will come true at their appointed time.' (vv. 19–20, NIV)

These words were spoken to Elizabeth's doubting husband, the priest Zechariah, on the day he was surprised by an angel while on duty in the temple in Jerusalem, burning the incense. The angel made a massive proclamation: Zechariah and his wife Elizabeth would have a son, and not just any son, but one who would be filled with the Holy Spirit, bring people back to God and prepare the way 'for the Lord'. What an announcement! After 400 years of silence from heaven, Gabriel himself was sent to usher in a completely new era of history.

But Zechariah was sceptical. And so, he was struck dumb. His silence was not chosen but imposed. Not so his wife Elizabeth, who was delighted with her ensuing pregnancy and gave all the glory to God: 'The Lord has done this for me' (v. 25). The five months she then spent in joyful solitude must surely have been weeks of gratitude and anticipation – such a gracious response to the gift she had received. She did not take her coming baby as a right or something she deserved. Rather, she treasured the season she was in and gave thanks to God. She had had some tough times in the past (v. 25) but was thoroughly appreciative of blessing now. She readied herself as well for the resistance of family to her baby's name, John, which would be out of step with family tradition, and for speaking up in public (v. 60). It seems that the wordless Zechariah learned his lesson too, for his first response when released from silence was to endorse his wife's words and praise his God.

Dear Father, help me to see and give thanks for your amazing blessings, even in tough times, but especially in good times. Let me joyfully give you thanks and praise and not be silent. Let me savour your kindness. Amen.

DI ARCHER

Coming together

'Blessed is she who has believed that the Lord would fulfil his promises
to her!' And Mary said: 'My soul glorifies the Lord and my spirit rejoices
in God my Saviour, for he has been mindful of the humble state of his
servant.' (vv. 45–48, NIV)

This is such a glorious moment in the story of the imminent arrival of the
man who would change the world. I love that his mother Mary went to see
her relation Elizabeth – indeed, she hurried there (v. 39). What a meeting
those two clearly had! It must have been profoundly happy and incredible.
Elizabeth was full of rejoicing again, and then Mary too, voicing a song
of praise that has been repeated countless times, in countless places, on
countless lips since, as the Magnificat. How must they have felt – knowing they were part of something extraordinary, yet not knowing how that
would be? Both were held steady by their trust in God, forged by Elizabeth
through solitude and by Mary through obedience.

It was now a time for getting together and the two women drew each
other closer to God. Solitude is not always the answer to the pivotal points
in life. I am sure this encounter was a profound encouragement to both
women, and they would need that reassurance in the amazing and the difficult days to come. Had they not spent time together with God, we would
not have the Magnificat; we would not know that the unborn baby John
had responded to the unborn baby Jesus – and how amazing that was.

These women knew that this was not the time for being alone, and that
they needed each other. Solitude has its place, but community does too.
We are made for both, and sometimes we have to be intentional about
reaching out to others when either we, or they, need it. If that feels hard,
then it probably means it's important to do.

---

*Read Matthew 18:19–20. It's all too easy to hang back from connection with
others out of shyness, reticence or busyness. How can you make meeting with
fellow believers more of a priority in your life?*

DI ARCHER

75

Jesus, master of silence and solitude

Very early in the morning, while it was still dark, Jesus got up, left the house and went off to a solitary place, where he prayed. Simon and his companions went to look for him, and when they found him, they exclaimed: 'Everyone is looking for you!' (vv. 35–37, NIV)

Jesus always made time with God a priority. Again and again, the gospels record that Jesus went off to pray alone. He would get up early to do it, stay up late to do it, avoid crowds to do it, refuse invitations to do it, irritate people to do it and leave his disciples to do it. It never feels like that was a chore or a duty, but rather was something he chose to do because he both wanted and needed to.

People saw the effect of that. It meant that he took the presence of God with him wherever he went. He claimed to know what the Father did, and what the Father wanted him to do (John 5:19–20). He said that he was really, really close to him (10:30). He said that doing what God wanted gave him strength beyond food (4:34). He said that we could see the Father in him (14:9). Everything about Jesus stems from his relationship with God.

The Christian tradition of silence and solitude took its inspiration from Jesus' example and has developed over the centuries since. It has expressed itself in myriad ways, from hermits and mystics to cloistered communities and retreats. Jesus showed that a deep relationship with God is a dynamic, loving, joyful and frankly mind-blowing possibility. And all that was available to Jesus is now available to us. What might we be missing by neglecting to spend time in silence and solitude?

Dear Father, please draw me closer to you. I want to know you more, trust you more and enjoy you more. Thank you for your kindness. Amen.

DI ARCHER

Finding strength in solitude

After he had dismissed [the crowd], he went up on a mountainside by himself to pray. Later that night, he was there alone, and the boat was already a considerable distance from land, buffeted by the waves because the wind was against it. (vv. 23–24, NIV)

Jesus had had a long day – and a long night lay ahead of him. The day had begun with the terrible news that his cousin John the Baptist had been beheaded by Herod Antipas. Jesus tried to find some privacy to respond to this, withdrawing to have time to himself and to spend with his Father God, but the crowd worked out where his boat was headed and greeted him on the shore. Amazingly, Jesus saw their need and put aside his grief to heal and show compassion (v. 14). He then fed them all, miraculously, with the help of his disciples. Finally, he got some peace to pray, by escaping up into the mountain.

We are not told about that prayer time, but it must have been agonised. I don't imagine that Jesus spent the whole session calmly sitting and receiving from God. As fully human, surely he would have had a significant, physical outpouring of grief. Perhaps, like me on a lone dog walk, he shouted into the wind and cried into his hands. Perhaps he threw a few rocks about. Perhaps he keeled over, feeling the loss of his loved cousin and knowing that he was headed in the same direction.

Somehow, Jesus processed his grief enough to be able to respond to his panicking disciples as they struggled to keep their boat steady against the opposing wind. He was able to perform his second outstanding miracle of the day, as he walked on the water to rescue them, caught hold of the sinking Peter, and demonstrated God's power and compassion all at once. He was able to do all these things because he stuck close to his Father.

Read John 14:12. What might God do through your life if you stick close to him, even through the distressing times?

DI ARCHER

Jesus – who is he?

Once when Jesus was praying in private and his disciples were with him, he asked them, 'Who do the crowds say I am?' They replied, 'Some say John the Baptist; others say Elijah...' 'But what about you?' he asked. 'Who do you say I am?' Peter answered, 'God's Messiah.'
(vv. 18–20, NIV)

It is notable how the gospel writers record how often Jesus prayed before – and after – significant events in his life. He clearly went to God for guidance on what he wanted him to do and when. Decisions, directions, locations, timings, miracles, teaching, healings, Jesus was obedient to his Father in them all. The gospel writer Luke is especially dedicated to reminding us of how Jesus' ministry revolved around his prayer times with God.

On this occasion, Jesus asked his disciples the key question about himself – and they reported back the same answers as were on the lips of many, including those reporting to Herod. Jesus asked this question in Caesarea Philippi, which was outside Herod's jurisdiction, so it was a slightly safer place to have this discussion. It may have given Peter the freedom to name Jesus as the Messiah and given Jesus the freedom to talk about the difficult days that lay ahead.

Jesus spoke previously about our need to be as 'shrewd as snakes and as innocent as doves' (Matthew 10:16). In giving his disciples strict instructions to keep Peter's remarkable revelation to themselves, he was keeping ahead of the dangerous enemies accumulating around him. As the political storm clouds gathered, he chose his moments and movements ever more carefully and always in communion with God.

As we follow in his footsteps, we cannot be naïve – there will be forces ranged against us. It can be that our most significant encounters with God happen in the middle of great crises and trouble. It is here that his compassion and kindness mean the most to us. So, keep in step with Jesus, for he is always ahead of the game and master of the storm.

Dear Father, I really don't like the storms in life, but please help me to hang on to you, trust you to get me through and see your deliverance. Thank you. Amen.

DI ARCHER

How to pray like Jesus

One day Jesus was praying in a certain place. When he finished, one of his disciples said to him, 'Lord, teach us to pray, just as John taught his disciples.' He said to them, 'When you pray, say: "Father, hallowed be your name, your kingdom come…"' (vv. 1–2, NIV)

There he was, praying again. It really was the bedrock and centre point of Jesus' life. No wonder, then, that one day the disciples asked him to teach them to pray. Thank goodness they did! Because of their curiosity and courage, we have the Lord's Prayer, which is still recited worldwide over 2,000 years later.

The Lord's Prayer gives us firm ground to stand on when we come to pray. The key is that first word: 'Father'. Jesus was not following in the Jewish tradition in using this familiar term for God. Jews would not have addressed God in this way. It was unheard of. They would have regarded it as irreverent and presumptuous. The Aramaic 'Abba' that Jesus used in the garden of Gethsemane was even more informal (Matthew 26:39). It would have been a revelation to the disciples, too, representing as it did the close relationship that Jesus had with God. It is a family term. It is for a son talking to his father, without fear, knowing he is accepted and welcome.

The rest of the Lord's Prayer flows from that one word. When we ask for provision, for sins to be forgiven, for protection from evil, we do so on the basis that we, like Jesus, are part of the family. We belong. Our Father is delighted to see and hear us. We can rush in to him – we do not need to hang back for any reason.

So, when you pick your places and times for silence and solitude to be with God, do not stand on ceremony. Get to him as quickly as possible. He is always waiting for you.

Read Isaiah 49:15–16. You may not always be thinking of God the Father, but he is always aware of you.

DI ARCHER

True love: 1 Corinthians 13

Jane Walters writes…

A quick Google search confirmed what I suspected: 1 Corinthians 13 is the most quoted reading at weddings. Where else in the Bible can we find such an outpouring of love's virtues? Yet its value should not be confined to the narrow context of marriage, as we shall explore over the next seven days.

It is always helpful to consider a biblical text's background. Paul was writing to the church he had founded in Corinth, a Roman colony located at the crossroads of a major sea route. Its culture was thereby influenced by the through traffic of other countries, and its population was cosmopolitan, with multiple expressions of religious beliefs and practices. Intellectual snobbery was rife, as was sexual depravity. Although the church was newly established, there were already deep-seated issues which Paul urgently needed to address. He was particularly concerned with the amount of division and sectarianism and the level of sexual immorality, which flagrantly disregarded Christ's call to holy living.

It seems to me that the references to love serve to pull together Paul's exhortations in the rest of his letter to live according to the gospel. Within a true understanding of what love demands is a call to look up – to look away from ourselves and each other and up at Jesus Christ, the head of the body, the church.

I wonder if, like me, you have ever been encouraged to substitute your own name for the word 'love'? We might read: 'Jane is patient, Jane is kind, etc.' It can provide a bit of a wake-up call when we do, but I feel it misses a point. We don't want to be thinking about love in a limited, human setting, bringing our understanding of love down to our level. Instead, we want to expand our thinking and challenge our attitudes. It is better, then, to substitute the name of Jesus for 'love' – after all, the Bible teaches us so clearly that God is love, through and through. And so, let us be encouraged to lift our eyes away from our circumstances, away from our preferred ways, and to consider how we can aim instead to follow in Jesus' footsteps. After all, he showed in word and deed, in attitude and behaviour, what it truly means to love.

Hollow words need a love-filling

**If I speak in the tongues of men or of angels, but do not have love,
I am only a resounding gong or a clanging cymbal. If I have the gift of
prophecy and can fathom all mysteries and all knowledge, and if I have
a faith that can move mountains, but do not have love, I am nothing.
(vv. 1–2, NIV)**

Some years ago, a friend recommended *The Five Love Languages* by
Gary Chapman. She had recently read it and had experienced something
of a revelation in her marriage. She had always been annoyed that her
husband preferred to clean her car than hug her. He would repeatedly
tell her that he loved her, but it felt meaningless without the actions she
expected him to make. All of that faded away, though, when she read how
'acts of service' was his way of showing her love, whereas she received love
through 'physical touch'. (I thoroughly recommend the book!)

In our relationships, we must guard against two equal and opposite
situations: speaking words of love that are empty of meaning or lacking
evidence; and acting in ways that lack love. If you've ever done a task for
someone when your heart isn't in it, you'll know that when love is absent,
resentment and even anger can be present. In the days when I found my
mother very difficult, I would busy myself helping her – telling myself I was
'honouring my father and mother' – but inside my blood would be boiling.
I tried to correct my attitude, kept biting my tongue, but in the end I simply
prayed that God would give me more love for her. It led to some painfully
honest conversations and a genuine exchange of forgiveness. I'm so grateful that, by the time she went to glory, our relationship was no longer one
which went through the motions but was truly love-filled.

See what a difference it makes to turn these verses around: 'When I have
the gift of prophecy/fathom all mysteries/give all I possess to the poor/give
over my body to hardship *and have love*, I gain *everything*.'

---

*Father, I ask that you create a new heart in me, with new hope and new love,
as I serve you. I choose to let go of all ill-feeling as you fill me afresh through
your Holy Spirit. Amen.*

JANE WALTERS

81

Love takes a lifetime to grow

Love is patient, love is kind. It does not envy, it does not boast, it is not proud. (NIV)

Reading this chapter out loud, I find myself slowing down at today's verse, like I'm unwittingly leaving space for the words that seem to be missing: 'love *should be* patient, love *should be* kind…' Certainly, these qualities seem in painfully short supply in our broken world. How do we bridge the gap between the ideal and the reality?

We soon find we cannot be patient or kind or avoid envy, boasting and pride by willpower alone. If you've ever made a resolution, at New Year or other times, you'll know the agony of finding that you simply cannot sustain the pace of your initial enthusiasm. This verse from the Old Testament is a huge help: '"Not by might nor by power, but by my Spirit," says the Lord Almighty' (Zechariah 4:6). Where our willpower is finite and all too limited, God's Holy Spirit is an ever-available source of God's very essence, which is, of course, love.

In my first career as a retailer, I employed a new part-time member of staff. The interview had gone well, and she was keen to join the team. There was only one problem: as soon as she started the job, I realised I didn't get on with her. I felt irritated by her perfectly reasonable questions; I saw her carefulness as a lack of confidence. I spent so many hours praying about it but to no avail. Sadly, she gave up and moved on. My determination to be different each working day simply wasn't enough.

Developing as a disciple of Jesus Christ takes a lifetime. There are no short cuts, no quick fixes. We will make many mistakes and hurt many people. The only answer is to plug more deeply into God, allowing him to transform us by the power of his Holy Spirit.

Lord, thank you that you are patient with us, bearing with us as we fail. Fill us with your Holy Spirit, that your loving attributes would grow as naturally as fruit, for the sake of others and for your glory. Amen.

JANE WALTERS

It's not about me!

[Love] does not dishonour others, it is not self-seeking, it is not easily angered, it keeps no record of wrongs. (NIV)

The challenges of this chapter continue, with a wider swipe at our society's culture. There is a whole generation being brought up within a culture of 'me, me, me'. The camera lens is literally turned towards us. Our focus tends not to be an outward one. The mantra is not so much 'If it feels good, do it', but 'Only do it if it makes you feel good.'

Self-seeking is the very antithesis of love. The marriage service offers a helpful illustration within the words spoken as the bride and groom exchange the rings: 'All that I am I give to you, and all that I have I share with you.' This opening of the hands and heart to each other is not so we receive, but rather give – and the attitude behind that is a complete, self-less, not-counting-the-cost kind of giving. How this world needs to see love like this! How we need to be people who answer the call to live like this!

In our relationships and dealings with people, forgiveness is one of the most powerful acts of love. Too often, when we feel wronged or aggrieved, we can sense anger flaring up and, before we know it, we have spoken out words that ought never to have been said. If we are honest with ourselves, it is our pride that has been hurt. Our hearts can be fragile, it is true; but we really mustn't employ pride as a kind of bodyguard to protect it. When we do, we find it all the harder to meaningfully connect with others and love has, once more, been sidelined.

Instead, let's be people who learn to honour others, to swallow down our pride-fuelled anger, to forgive, then let go. Let love show us a better way.

Are you struggling to forgive someone? Think about the many ways Jesus has forgiven you. Ask him for more grace, so you can stop re-reading your records of wrongs and, in an ultimately selfless act, forgive them from your heart.

JANE WALTERS

Watch your mouth

Love does not delight in evil but rejoices with the truth. It always protects, always trusts, always hopes, always perseveres. (NIV)

'Love does not delight in evil.' If we follow the suggestion I mentioned in the introduction and state instead, 'Jane does not delight in evil', I would nod my head in agreement. Why on earth would I choose to side with evil? Perhaps you had the same (self-righteous) response when using your own name. However, let us pause; take a moment to be honest with ourselves.

Oscar Wilde famously said that the only thing worse than being talked about was not being talked about, but gossip is not funny and it's not loving. Stand at a bus stop, walk around a supermarket or spend time in a staffroom and you will hear people talking about other people. Tune your ear into the detail. Are they talking positively? Most likely, they are taking the opportunity to be catty, drawing further vindictiveness from their audience. Half the time, their information is second- or third-hand, a twisting of misinformation that results in rumours and gossip spreading like wildfire.

Far worse is when gossip happens in our church communities. 'Have you heard about so-and-so…?' 'Just for prayer, are you aware that…?' I have all too often been privy to information that simply wasn't mine to know, and it's so hard to discern the best way to respond, and I've had to reassure myself that at least having reached me, it will go no further.

Paul states that love 'always protects' – let us apply that to people's privacy; 'always trusts' – that what we say in confidence remains in confidence; 'always hopes' – that people will believe the best about us and give us the benefit of the doubt; and 'always perseveres' – let us be those who swim against the current, refusing to be swept along by the gossipy tide.

Have you been subjected to gossip? Bring the pain to Jesus, who can heal you and help you forgive. Have you indulged in gossip, either by speaking or listening? Repent, receive forgiveness and pledge to do it no more.

JANE WALTERS

This is now and that is then

Love never fails. But where there are prophecies, they will cease; where there are tongues, they will be stilled; where there is knowledge, it will pass away. For we know in part and we prophesy in part, but when completeness comes, what is in part disappears. (NIV)

In one sense, these verses make for curious reading. Paul has extolled the virtues of spiritual gifts in the previous chapter – and will go on to encourage prophecy in the next, but he's not intending to diminish their importance here. Rather, he is showing us the truer perspective: that they are indeed valuable, but only for a time.

When my husband and I were dating, we regularly sent each other WhatsApp messages whenever we were apart. Several times a day, and especially first thing in the morning and last thing at night, we would pour our hearts out on to our phone screens. Keen never to lose this record, he printed them all out – hundreds of pages of tiny text! Now that we are married, it has mostly stopped, but that does not mean we have stopped loving each other; it's simply that the moment has moved on, while the love has remained.

Cessationists would assert that the gifts of the Holy Spirit stopped after the time of the apostles. This is not what Paul is maintaining here. Just as my husband and I stopped texting each other when we were able to say it all face-to-face, so these gifts of prophecy, speaking in tongues and having words of knowledge as ways of communicating with God, and on behalf of him, will one day not be required, because we will see him face-to-face. Hallelujah! What a glorious day that will be!

We need, therefore, to avoid falling into both traps, neither venerating the gifts so highly that we can't see their temporary nature nor dismissing them as unimportant just because one day they will fade away. This is now; that is then.

Spend some time thinking ahead to the day you will see God face-to-face. What would you like to say to him? How will it feel? Thank him for the reality of that hope and the enduring nature of love.

JANE WALTERS

Maturing is not optional

When I was a child, I talked like a child, I thought like a child, I reasoned like a child. When I became a man, I put the ways of childhood behind me. For now we see only a reflection as in a mirror; then we shall see face to face. Now I know in part; then I shall know fully, even as I am fully known. (NIV)

I'm a big fan of childhood. Who doesn't want to spend their time playing, coming in to find food already prepared and being tucked up in bed when you're tired? I'm feeling quite wistful just thinking about it. I remember when my younger son was in year four at primary school, complaining that he just wanted to play in the sandpit as he had in reception.

The fact is, for most of us, growing up is something we cannot avoid – and with good reason! We are hard-wired to mature, to develop, to be stretched emotionally, mentally and physically. It is all part of God's 'very good' plan of creation. But how about maturing spiritually? Earlier in this letter, Paul has berated the Corinthian church for their childish behaviour – demonstrated in their divisions and factions – and bemoaned that 'I gave you milk, not solid food, for you were not yet ready for it. Indeed, you are still not ready' (3:2).

The process of growing up inevitably involves discarding childish things. The things you adorned your younger self's bedroom with – David Cassidy posters, anyone? – are hardly appropriate now. What of our spiritual habits? So much of this chapter has pointed to our need to change. Children are famously self-absorbed, acting like the universe revolves around them. They are notoriously impatient: 'Are we there yet?' Surely, we wouldn't want to be stuck in those behaviours, would we?

I want to suggest that it is Christ's love for us that compels us to leave our old ways behind. As surely as he said to the disciples, 'Follow me,' and they abandoned their nets and were drawn into their faith adventure, so too can we experience the fullness of new life if we just let go.

Has anything in today's reading or notes particularly challenged you? Is there something practical you can do in response? What can you let go of? What is God calling you to take up?

JANE WALTERS

What remains

And now these three remain: faith, hope and love. But the greatest of these is love. (NIV)

Yesterday's thoughts centred around the changes that occur as we mature and develop as people and believers. We naturally jettison things along the way, whether that's physical possessions or more personal, internal things. Eventually, all the 'stuff' fades away until what remains is distilled down to the very essence of life, into what's truly important: faith, hope and love.

I have in mind the settlers who panned for gold in the 19th century. Many had travelled in great hope of a better life, even a prosperous one. They believed the reports and had faith that they were true. They endured long hours of sifting through soil, silt and mud, examining it, peering in for the slightest glimpse of the precious metal whose discovery would transform their lives. When all the muck was washed away, they were left with something that would never rust or tarnish or, for that matter, lose its value.

In a real sense, we too are spending our days panning for gold. Job learned the truth of this. In his intense suffering and extreme loss, he was able to say of God: 'He knows the way that I take; when he has tested me, I will come forth as gold' (Job 23:10). Throughout his trials, when he was all but reduced to nothing, Job's faith and hope in God prevailed until the day when God revealed himself and lovingly rewarded him.

Forget the Hollywood image of a couple promising to love each other forever. Sometimes love looks more like the gold with its mud and silt still clinging: sleepless nights caring for someone, washing the feet of the homeless, getting our hands dirty for love's sake, demonstrating that love's enduring, transforming power is priceless.

God, what can we say in response to your amazing love? Thank you that you love us unconditionally and for all eternity. May we show your love to all we meet today, spreading hope and encouraging faith. Amen.

JANE WALTERS

Women in the early church

Naomi Aidoo writes…

The history of women in the Bible and in the building of God's kingdom is a complicated one. There are many schools of thought regarding what women could have, should have and did contribute. One thing is clear: Jesus' heart for women is that we are to flourish and thrive in him, living life to the full. This begins with abiding in him, and where better to do that than God's word?

There are countless stories in the Bible of women boldly and courageously building God's kingdom. However, kingdom building takes on many different shapes and forms: serving, prayer, working, parenting, friendship, teaching, giving and more. It's safe to say that the advancement and growth of the early church wasn't based on preaching and teaching alone. As well as the word being taught, countless men and women listened to God's call and filled gaps others couldn't, which led to significant impact.

As Christian women today, there are many seasons of life where we might feel as though our contribution to building the kingdom pales into insignificance in comparison to others. I've personally had moments when my biggest achievement on any given day has felt like making it out of the house with two fully dressed little people in tow. This barely even seems noteworthy when looking around at others. In those moments, it can be all too easy to fall into the comparison trap and believe that those we're watching are making contributions which are more important than ours. This a lie which, when believed, can lead us to climb into something we're not called to do.

The purpose of this study, as we journey into the lives of some of the women in the early church, is to recognise that there is beauty and power in contributing to God's kingdom in various ways. My prayer as you read is that you'll recognise yourself in these words and understand how significant your contribution to building God's kingdom is and continually will be as you abide in him – whatever that looks like.

Leaving a legacy: Tabitha

Peter went with them, and when he arrived he was taken upstairs to the room. All the widows stood around him, crying and showing him the robes and other clothing that Dorcas had made while she was still with them. (v. 39, NIV)

When precious people pass away, it's wonderful, albeit emotional, to hear their loved ones talk about the sort of person they were and the type of things they did. Tabitha (or Dorcas, as she was called in Greek) was no exception.

Peter had been called, it seems, in the hopes that he would be able to bring this woman who had died back to life. This sort of request isn't exactly the norm nowadays, is it? What does that say then of the faith-filled culture and atmosphere which Tabitha had once inhabited – or perhaps even contributed to creating? It was a time when the power of the Holy Spirit was made manifest, and the supernatural wasn't necessarily out of the ordinary. When Tabitha's friends heard that Peter was in town, they didn't think twice about asking him to come, even though Tabitha was already dead (v. 37).

In verse 36, we read that she was 'always doing good and helping the poor'. How might her friends communicate this legacy of a lifetime to a man who knew nothing about her? In verse 39 we see this question answered as these friends show Peter the robes and clothing she had made – evidence of the stories they would no doubt be sharing. Why was this clothing significant? Were these some of the garments she had made in order to clothe the poor?

Tabitha was brought back to life. But before this happened, her legacy was brought to the attention of both the friends who had journeyed with her and also to this stranger who had been called to her in haste. Her legacy was known, and her legacy was shown.

I thank you, Lord, that despite our time on earth being short, you've given us character, gifts and skills which contribute to creating a legacy. I pray that when it's our time to go, our legacy will point to you. Amen.

NAOMI AIDOO

89

Hands and heart: Lydia

One of those listening was a woman from the city of Thyatira named Lydia, a dealer in purple cloth. She was a worshipper of God. The Lord opened her heart to respond to Paul's message. (v. 14, NIV)

Although not much is said about Lydia, the fact that she was the first of Paul's converts is significant. She is described as 'a dealer in purple cloth'. Only the very wealthy were able to buy and wear purple cloth, due to the type of expensive dye used on the garments, so this indicates that Lydia was a wealthy businesswoman.

Despite no doubt being busy with constant demands and requests as she traded this costly cloth, we read that she had made time to pray with some other women (v. 13). So often the busyness and the business of this world creep in to distract and even deter us from making time for God, but here is Lydia, ensuring that despite those demands, prayer is prioritised. As believers living in the 21st century, with a constant bombardment of notifications from our phones alone, this should certainly serve as a reminder that carving out time to sit at the feet of Jesus is non-negotiable.

Luke describes Lydia as a worshipper of God. Many believe this to mean that in almost every sense of the word, she carried herself as if she were a Jew. We read that God opened her heart, which is what's key here. However, Lydia also made the provision to be there and to listen, taking on the disposition of a learner. This is where we must take note as leaders in our life and work. With God, there's no hierarchy. Yes, we each have unique gifts, which he's given us the grace to use. But, just like Lydia, before we get there, we must be willing to lay aside any ego or pride and simply sit at his feet.

What is our rhythm of reflection and worship amid our busy lives? Are we prioritising prayer and fellowship with fellow believers? Is there anything we can do to help this become more of a norm?

NAOMI AIDOO

Leadership through various lenses: Priscilla

They arrived at Ephesus, where Paul left Priscilla and Aquila. He himself went into the synagogue and reasoned with the Jews. (v.19, NIV)

As well as here in the book of Acts, Priscilla and Aquila are also mentioned in Romans, 1 Corinthians and 2 Timothy. It's therefore no surprise that they're commonly regarded as significant figures in the early church. Unusually, Priscilla's name is mentioned before her husband Aquila's, which leads many scholars to suggest that she was of more significance as a leader during this time than Aquila. The order that names are given in the Bible is important, something we know from the biblical interpretation of the 'law of first mention'. However, more on this later. What did this power pair actually do to warrant such prominence in God's word?

Verses 24–26 introduce us to a man named Apollos, who is described as a 'learned man' and a bold speaker. The text goes on to say that although he taught accurately, he knew only the baptism of John and had not yet heard the whole message of Jesus. When Priscilla and Aquila notice this, they don't snigger behind his back, considering themselves superior teachers. Nor do they publicly make mention of it. Instead, they invite him back to their house to explore and explain things more thoroughly.

Also note how at this point in his ministry journey, Paul was travelling with both Priscilla and Aquila. It makes me wonder if Paul, whom we know later wrote a great deal about marriage despite being unmarried himself, was taking notes as he lived alongside Priscilla and Aquila? Leadership and roles can be seen through a variety of lenses, not only in our work, but in the entirety of our lives.

Lord, may our leadership reflect your values and kingdom principles regardless of our own cultural and societal norms. Amen.

NAOMI AIDOO

Labour of love: Euodia and Syntyche

Yes, and I ask you, my true companion, help these women since they have contended at my side in the cause of the gospel, along with Clement and the rest of my co-workers, whose names are in the book of life. (v. 3, NIV)

When I remember my days as a secondary school teacher, I'm reminded of both the fondness and the frustration which could arise on any given day. I often referred to it as a 'labour of love'. I most certainly saw and knew the significance of what I was doing when I worked with some of the most vulnerable students in our school, but this by no means meant I found it easy. Yes, there were definitely times when I thoroughly enjoyed my work, but there were also times when I'd cry on my husband's shoulder before even leaving the house.

It's for those reasons that I understand Paul's use of the word 'contended' when describing Euodia and Syntyche's work alongside him 'in the cause of the gospel'. The Greek root word of this phrase 'contended' or 'laboured with' is *sunathleō*, which literally means to 'wrestle in company with' or to 'strive together for'. At first glance, some might find this sort of statement difficult. The notion that working with and for Jesus can be hard is not something we want to hear. Some believers wrongly associate coming to Christ with an easy life. The truth is Jesus tells us that in this world we will have trouble (John 16:33), but he also tells us that he's overcome the world.

It's with this knowledge that I believe Euodia and Syntyche laboured alongside Paul, despite their own personal disagreements, which Paul seems to highlight here. They knew the truth of Christ and the importance of ensuring his gospel was preached, no matter what.

Are there areas of your life where you are currently finding it challenging to stay committed? May the lives and labours of these women cause us to continue in our calling for the sake of Christ.

NAOMI AIDOO

Parenting the next generation in faith: Lois and Eunice

I am reminded of your sincere faith, which first lived in your grand-mother Lois and in your mother Eunice and, I am persuaded, now lives in you also. (v. 5, NIV)

There have been more times than I can remember in recent years when I have stood in the foyer of my church rocking a restless baby or tending to a toddler. When my children have needed some extra support in certain moments, I've found myself pacing the carpeted floor, re-reading the same notice boards and silently hoping I might soon be able to re-enter the service.

There was one day, however, when my attention was drawn to the stained-glass-window-style pictures at the back of the foyer. Each of the four pictures displayed biblical 'greats' (Timothy, John the Baptist, Samuel and Isaac) as children with their parents and/or grandparents. It's easy to overlook Lois, Eunice, Zechariah, Elizabeth, Hannah, Elkanah and Sarah (perhaps not so easy to overlook Abraham, but you get my point!) and yet these were parents raising the next generation and trusting the Lord to guide them. That thought brought me great encouragement that Sunday.

Most of these parents and grandparents had less notable roles than those of their children, but their legacies and stories are evident in the pages of scripture. If, for example, Lois and Eunice hadn't been willing to put the time and effort into discipling Timothy, he wouldn't have had the faith he came to have, which impacted so many, and he may not have even had a faith at all – who knows?

Being a mum of two young children myself, I don't doubt that Eunice and Lois would have faced difficulties as they brought up Timothy. Yet, even today, we are reaping the benefits of their ministry as we read of Timothy's life and service.

Lord, as we raise the next generation in faith – whether our children, grand-children, relatives or those in our churches and communities – remind us that we don't do it alone, but that you have gone before us. Amen.

NAOMI AIDOO

Standing up and standing out: Phoebe and Junia

I commend to you our sister Phoebe, a deacon of the church in Cenchreae… Greet Andronicus and Junia, my fellow Jews who have been in prison with me. They are outstanding among the apostles, and they were in Christ before I was. (vv. 1, 7, NIV)

I'll never forget the time I was working on a church staff team and we invited a coach to come and do some leadership training. The purpose of the training was to discover our leadership 'voice', unpacking why some people always seemed more vocal than others and vice versa. After a long day of questions asked and answered, it became clear that my leadership voice is what's known as a 'Pioneer'. Pioneers are the least representative of the thousands who have taken the test, especially among women. Although I've since learned to embrace my slight differences or the ways in which my personality might go against the 'norm', there have certainly been times when I have felt uncomfortable.

Today, there continues to be many differing views regarding women in church leadership positions. It's hard to know whether Phoebe, described as a church deacon, or Junia, 'outstanding amongst the apostles' at the very least (some would even say she was an apostle), had any difficulty accepting and embracing the prominent roles they held. Whatever attitudes they faced, they embraced the calling bestowed upon them and effected change in many people's lives as a result. In Phoebe's case, Paul went a step further, ensuring that the people provided her with whatever help and support she needed (v. 2).

When jealousy and uncertainty are left unchecked, it can cause all sorts of problems. Here were two women able to put their potential fear, questions and maybe even criticism aside for the sake of the gospel. May we confidently be able to do the same.

Have you ever felt that the role you're holding at work, in ministry or anywhere else doesn't quite fit the 'norm'? Pray that you will feel free to embrace who and whose you are, exactly where you are.

NAOMI AIDOO

From least to leader: Mary Magdalene

The twelve were with him, and also some women who had been cured of evil spirits and diseases: Mary (called Magdalene) from whom seven demons had come out. (vv.1-2, NIV)

Some people struggle to let go of the past. We might talk about how God can take our sins 'like scarlet' and make them 'white as snow' (Isaiah 1:18), but are we living in that truth? Have we wholeheartedly embraced the new life we have received through Christ? Mary Magdalene was someone who was able to do just that.

The gospels of Mark and Luke both share accounts of Mary's demon possession, which is what we read of her being freed from in today's passage. Women were already treated as inferior during this time, so we can only imagine the shame and shunning Mary faced from society as she struggled to live, possessed by demons she had no control over.

She lived that life among the same people she now saw as she followed Jesus boldly, even contributing to his ministry financially. She didn't shy away for fear of what others might think or say as this woman, once lost and least, now walked alongside Jesus as one of his closest companions. She knew that Jesus no longer saw her as she used to be, and so why should she? We don't know what others might have thought and said as she walked past them alongside women who were more highly esteemed. To Mary, it didn't matter. All she knew was that the demons who once possessed her life were now gone, and what she was called to today was of much greater significance.

We can learn so much from Mary Magdalene. We too are all new creations in Christ, despite what our past has been. May we learn to lead in the new life Jesus has given us, rather than operating as though our old identities still apply. Jesus has the final say.

Lord, please help me to live in the light of the new life you have given. Help me to forget the former things and to walk in the truth that you have set me free for good. Amen.

NAOMI AIDOO

Maximising means: Joanna and Susanna

Joanna the wife of Chuza, the manager of Herod's household; Susanna; and many others. These women were helping to support them out of their own means. (v. 3, NIV)

Although we read much of this passage yesterday, we couldn't move on without also acknowledging the significance of the other two named women – Joanna and Susanna. I say 'named women' because this verse indicates that there were in fact many other women walking with Jesus during this time. That in and of itself is noteworthy.

Perhaps even more startling, then, is that these women were not only following Jesus, but they also played crucial roles in supporting his ministry. Not much is said about Susanna and Joanna specifically, but what we do know is that both women were wealthy and used their money to support Jesus. We know from the previous verse that they were once held captive by evil spirits and diseases. How like our God for him to ensure that those once meant for evil were now contributing to the advancement of the kingdom!

Some Christians falsely believe that having faith and financial means simultaneously is somehow to be frowned upon. This couldn't be further from the truth. When scripture talks about money being the root of all evil, it's the *love* of money which is the problem rather than the money itself (1 Timothy 6:10).

If you're someone who runs a global business or has a busy corporate life, you might find yourself wondering how you can make an impact on the local church with what feels like limited time and capacity. Contributing to the financial costs of a ministry so it can still operate, and the people within it can do what they've been called to do without worry, is of immense value. It certainly was to Jesus.

Are you struggling to see how you can contribute to building the kingdom? What options come to mind when thinking outside of the box like Joanna and Susanna did?

NAOMI AIDOO

Working through conflict: Chloe

My brothers and sisters, some from Chloe's household have informed me that there are quarrels among you. (v. 11, NIV)

When we begin a new career or venture, we often idealise what it might look like and the impact we might have in the role. There are days when those dreams and bubbling anticipation appear to be fulfilled – a breakthrough with a difficult situation, a heart-warming email that lets you know what you're doing is making an impact – but there are also days when things don't go right and we come crashing back down to reality. Having to make hard decisions and have challenging conversations with people probably aren't top of our ideals list when we take on a new responsibility. Yet, it doesn't take long for us to find ourselves there.

This is what Chloe faced when the church group who met in her house had been arguing with one another. Scholars are divided on what it might mean that the church met in Chloe's house. Some say she'd have had spiritual authority, others that she'd simply opened her home so that people could gather there. Either way, I believe Chloe would have felt a weight of responsibility about the situation.

When we face difficulties or challenges, it can be easy (or at least easier) to question where God is in the midst of what's going on. Rather than throwing in the towel, it's crucial that we receive help and support. We don't know whether it was Chloe herself or those around her who wrote to Paul to ask for help, but either way, she wasn't left to her own devices. Instead, she had support around her as she followed her calling. This is certainly something for us to remember as we pursue our own calling.

Lord, please grant me the supernatural strength to be able to do what you've called me to. When times are testing and I'm not sure how to make sense of what I face, please surround me with the right people to help. Amen.

NAOMI AIDOO

Excited and insistent faith: Rhoda

When she recognised Peter's voice, she was so overjoyed she ran back without opening it and exclaimed, 'Peter is at the door!' (v. 14, NIV)

The whole of the first part of Acts 12 takes us on quite a journey. It begins with Peter being imprisoned and then subsequently being led out of the prison by an angel. What happens next reveals what was happening behind the scenes before the supernatural jailbreak.

In verse 5, we read that the church was gathered in Mary's home and praying for Peter's release. I wonder how many people were there. What would the conversations have been like? And how hopeful were they that their prayers would be answered?

There were so many people praying that a servant named Rhoda was there to answer the door. She may have been there to pray with the others and just happened to be the one to answer the door, but the fact that the passage makes mention of her occupation leads me to believe that she had been specifically enlisted for the job – an important and yet seemingly insignificant task.

How often, when we're so earnestly and zealously praying for something, do we believe it truly will come to pass? I'm not sure how often I believe the answers to my prayers will come knocking on my door! Yet that's exactly what happened here. Rhoda was in such shock, she forgot to let Peter in. The others couldn't believe what they were hearing ('What is this servant saying?', I imagine them asking) and needed some persuading, eventually going to the door to see for themselves!

When we are praying for something that appears to be impossible, may we be bold in our prayers and confident enough in Christ that we'll see it come to pass.

However insignificant and unimportant our day might seem, may we be drawn to the magnificent in the mundane and recognise that there is no circumstance too hard for God to break through.

NAOMI AIDOO

Working hard in the Lord: Tryphena, Tryphosa and Persis

Greet Tryphena and Tryphosa, those women who work hard in the Lord. Greet my dear friend Persis, another woman who has worked very hard in the Lord. (v. 12, NIV)

I wonder what image springs to mind when you picture the concept 'working hard in the Lord'. At one time in my life my mind would have most certainly gone to overseas missionary work, preaching and teaching from the pulpit, or being employed by a church or Christian organisation. In fact, these were the sort of roles I aspired to when I was younger because I believed that they were what real Christian work looked like.

Of course, I was wrong, and I was delighted to come to my senses through wise counsel and a more accurate understanding of what 'ministry' truly means. I've had the privilege of realising the presence of God in all manner of situations and conversations in my working life since those former years.

We don't know what kind of work Tryphena, Tryphosa and Persis were involved in; we're simply told that they worked hard in the Lord. Let's be encouraged by their example as we consider our various roles. Perhaps you're a teacher and you're using your ability to break down complicated concepts to enable students to better understand and progress in their studies. Maybe you work in retail and the knack you have to brighten a person's day by your attention to detail and customer service is how you work hard for the Lord.

The truth of the matter is that whatever your work or day-to-day role looks like, if you are trusting God to lead and guide your steps, you are very much in the company of Tryphena, Tryphosa and Persis, working hard in the Lord.

Father God, when I feel as though my work doesn't count for anything in terms of the kingdom, help me to remember these women and countless others who worked hard in the Lord regardless of their job title. Amen.

NAOMI AIDOO

Spiritual service: Nympha

Give my greetings to the brothers and sisters at Laodicea, and to Nympha and the church in her house. (v. 15, NIV)

Have you ever been to someone's house for a meal and been completely taken aback by their hospitality? I'm not talking about a lavish meal, but rather the host's warmth, attention to detail and care in the food they've prepared. You just know that they're genuinely happy you're sitting there with them. I've experienced this a few times and it's taught me that hospitality truly is a gift.

We don't know much about Nympha, but we know from Revelation 3:17–18 that the church in Laodicea was wealthy. It's for this reason that it's often inferred that Nympha was wealthy too. Certainly, in order to have a church meet in your house, you needed to have the means and the space to be able to do this.

While wealth is not a prerequisite for hospitality, the point here is that, like so many of the other wonderful women we've read of in this series, Nympha used what she had in order to be a blessing to the church. We don't know of her spiritual stature so far as teaching and preaching is concerned, but we do know that she was willing to open her home and in so doing she was able to contribute to the building of the kingdom.

When God met Moses, he asked him: 'What is that in your hand?' (Exodus 4:2). For Moses, it was a walking stick which was later used to part the Red Sea. For Nympha, it was her home, which she opened so that the church could meet. What's in our hands to give back to God?

Have you ever downplayed the resources you have (or perhaps don't have)? May today's passage be a refreshing reminder that God can use whatever you're willing to give.

NAOMI AIDOO

Prayer without ceasing: Anna

Coming up to them at that very moment, she gave thanks to God and spoke about the child to all who were looking forward to the redemption of Jerusalem. (v. 38, NIV)

One of my great loves is a live theatre production. As a performing arts degree graduate and an ex-drama teacher, there's something which stirs within me every time I get to watch a live show. I love to look at the actor's faces when they've finished singing their big number or when they're about to take their final bow and see that look which says: 'This is it! This is what it's all been for.' If we think about the hours of learning lines, rehearsal and everything in between which goes into making a live performance happen, it's no surprise to see that look of elation on the faces of the artists as we watch them perform.

However, these moments pale in comparison to Anna's experience as she recognises the infant Jesus as the king of kings she'd been speaking of and praying about for many years. He had finally arrived. To some perhaps, this was just another birth of another baby, but for Anna it was the fulfilment of years of prophesying and prayer. We read in verse 37 that she was a widow and that she never left the temple. After her husband died, it seems that she dedicated absolutely everything she had and was to sharing the news of the coming king.

The day Jesus was born changed everything for everyone, and Anna was able to see God's promise come to pass firsthand. We don't know exactly what Anna said here, but I imagine her standing beside Mary and Joseph as they held Jesus and internally breathing a sigh of relief. Her prayers had been answered and her prophecy fulfilled. The king had come!

Lord, I pray that Anna's example of prayer and dedication will inspire my own prayer life. Thank you for the privilege of being able to spend time with you. Amen.

NAOMI AIDOO

The power of friendship: Elizabeth

When Elizabeth heard Mary's greeting, the baby leaped in her womb, and Elizabeth was filled with the Holy Spirit. (v. 41, NIV)

The building of God's kingdom comes about through the work of countless committed Christians powerfully operating in their spheres of influence for the collective reward of seeing people come to Jesus. However, doing this work is never meant to be a solo endeavour.

Ever since becoming a mum, I've heard the phrase 'It takes a village to raise a child' countless times, and I can absolutely attest to it being true. Without the support and care of trusted family and friends, I wouldn't be the mum I want to be by any means. Parents seeking to raise spiritually mature children need the love, support and, most importantly, prayers of those around us to help.

If anyone needed a village it was Mary. This unknown teenager was called to carry God's own Son, to be his mother and care for him. Elizabeth, who Luke tells us was a relative of Mary, was certainly a formative part of Mary's village.

As if Mary wasn't already perplexed enough by the angel Gabriel's visit and the news she was given, she'd probably have been even more confused that her elderly relative was also pregnant. I wonder what greeting she anticipated as she approached Elizabeth's house.

Mary needn't have worried. When Elizabeth heard Mary's greeting, her own baby leapt in her womb, and she was filled with the Holy Spirit. If Mary was unsure before, after this visit with Elizabeth she no doubt had the confidence to know that this was a moment of huge significance both for now and forever. These two women were able to encourage each other as they rejoiced in what God was doing in their lives.

When we consider our Christian friendships, do we realise the significant part we play for each other in supporting one another's kingdom growth? Let's boldly encourage one another in our call in Christ.

NAOMI AIDOO

Jeremiah: the prophecies

Sara Batts-Neale writes…

Last month we spent a week with Jeremiah. We thought about what it means to be a prophet and the emotional and spiritual burden that that calling creates. In the week ahead, we're looking at the things Jeremiah did and said. What did his prophecies say, and how were they received? Who were his listeners, and what did they think of him?

The incidences recorded in Jeremiah aren't always chronological. That's one of the things that can make it a tricky book to read. It is also helpful to keep in mind the changing political background. In the early sixth century BC, Assyria lost its place as the dominant power in the region. Babylon, under Nebuchadnezzar, grew in power during this time. Judah, under King Josiah, was able to make religious reform a priority – but that didn't last long. After King Josiah died, reforms were forgotten – despite the prophet's warnings to his son – and disaster befell the people in the final days of the southern kingdom of Judah. People were exiled in several tranches, but in 586BC the temple was destroyed and Babylon ruled the roost. Jeremiah 40—43 outline the story of these years.

However, the exile isn't the end of the story. There is a hope of restoration – something that is prophesied throughout the book – and Jeremiah ends with a number of prophecies against the neighbouring nations. God reminds them, as it were, not to get too big for their boots. Babylon might have been the tool God used to show his anger with his people, but God is more powerful than Babylon.

When we look at the text, it's a rough rule of thumb that the prophecies as spoken are presented as poetry whereas the narrative is in prose. Through the centuries, poetry has been used to stir emotions, using images and metaphors to convey complex ideas. These prophecies are no different.

Our brief survey of the book of Jeremiah this week will show us how Jeremiah acted out his prophecies, how he was challenged and persevered, and the words he gave to the exiles and the remnant in Jerusalem. We'll jump about a bit, as we tackle foolishness, recalcitrance, underwear and the sabbath. It's not always a cheerful read, but we'll end with the joyful notes of hope and the new covenant we see fulfilled in Christ.

103

Faithful hearts

So I bought a loincloth according to the word of the Lord and put it on my loins (v. 2, NRSV)

What's your opinion of lingerie? Are you a practical, slightly saggy-pants kind of person or is yours all beautifully matched? I'd love to be the latter but have to admit that most of the time I'm the former. There's something special about having lovely things that others can't see – a pleasure for ourselves that we hold close. And it's that intimacy we reflect on for today's passage.

The story of the loincloth is one of Jeremiah's enacted parables – an action being performed, rather than a story being told. It was widely held that the act had a power to effect change in its own right. There's another example in chapter 27, where Jeremiah wears a yoke. In today's reading, Jeremiah reports that he was commanded by God to buy, wear and hide a loincloth. Upon retrieving it, the loincloth was ruined. That represents the rejection by the people of Israel and Judah. They were chosen by God to be on the most intimate terms with him, but they have rejected his words and his will and gone off to find their own gods.

What would life look like if we worked on the assumption that God wants us to be close to him at all times?

I think that wearing our nicest underwear makes us act differently on the outside. It's a confidence boost, perhaps, that makes us stand straighter, taller – to look people in the eye, to act more confidently. I'm going to stretch a metaphor here and hope it doesn't break like old pants' elastic: if we keep close to God, keep listening to Jesus in the quiet of our soul as part of our daily life, that will lead us to think and act differently. We have an inner life that influences our outer interactions with others, and that's how we show the beauty of a life lived with Christ.

'As God's chosen ones, holy and beloved, clothe yourselves with compassion, kindness, humility, meekness, and patience' (Colossians 3:12).

SARA BATTS-NEALE

Critical hearts

Thus says the Lord: Stand in the court of the Lord's house and speak to all the cities of Judah that come to worship in the house of the Lord. (v. 2, NRSV)

I have the privilege of preaching regularly, and I'm always a little anxious about how my words will land. So far, though, I've had few really critical comments, and nothing has landed me in court. Which is nothing like the reaction Jeremiah receives!

Back at the beginning of February, we read Jeremiah 7 together. Today we read a different perspective of the same 'temple sermon'. Chapter 26 summarises the general message – repent and recommit your ways to God or disaster will befall you – without going into as much detail. In this version, instead, we are given far more detail about the crowd's reaction. Jeremiah was preaching to the leaders of his day. He was setting himself against other prophets and religious authorities and, unsurprisingly, these people were incensed. They were so outraged at what he was saying that Jeremiah was put on trial, accused of prophesying against the city. Nothing like shooting the messenger when you're unhappy with the message!

This got me wondering about how we react to criticism. Does the quality of the message we receive depend on how well we think of the critic? It's quite likely we react better to criticism if we like those offering feedback. When we feel it's unjustified it's very tempting to assume we're definitely right and the other person is definitely wrong, become entrenched in our position and find it harder to listen with an open heart and mind.

Clear feedback, given kindly, can show us exactly where we are falling short – and we are all falling short, as Romans 3 tells us, so none of us can hide behind the idea we are already perfect. Where might we need to listen a bit more closely to the feedback we'd rather dismiss?

'If we say that we have no sin, we deceive ourselves, and the truth is not in us. If we confess our sins, he who is faithful and just will forgive us our sins and cleanse us from all unrighteousness' (1 John 1:8–9).

SARA BATTS-NEALE

Foolish hearts

'Hear this, O foolish and senseless people, who have eyes but do not see, who have ears but do not hear. Do you not fear me? says the Lord. (vv. 21–22, NRSV)

I really enjoy good April Fool's jokes – a bit of creative, kind silliness in an otherwise serious world. It's fun to try to spot the article written by someone like Lil P. O'Roaf, particularly if one is taken in by the subject matter first!

I don't often relish being called a fool, though. There is nothing gentle or silly about the foolishness in today's passage. Jeremiah tells us that at first, when no one listened, he assumed he was talking to foolish people – those without capacity for understanding. So he went instead to the leaders, who of course would know what their God required of them. He discovers this is not true. Fools abound. They have rejected the yoke of the covenant and been utterly unfaithful to God. That's one aspect to their foolishness. Another is their refusal to believe there will be any consequences, saying that the prophets are nothing more than wind to them. They have eyes but cannot see and ears but cannot hear – and that's the third kind of foolishness, the deliberate ignoring of the signs around them.

Jeremiah 5 sets out exactly why God is allowing the coming disaster. God knows his people will ask, 'Why has the Lord our God done all this to us?' and he gives Jeremiah a precise answer. Sadly, however, the people don't want to heed the warnings. They would rather stay in ignorance, doing what they want, than turn back to God and the precious covenant. So, the final kind of tragic foolishness lies in their stubborn hearts.

Stubbornness – and its cousin, pride – can stop us admitting we are wrong. They stop us admitting we have been fooled by wrong ideas or seductive temptation. Admitting our foolishness is the first step to true repentance. Can you be a fool today?

God of our laughter, we thank you for the moments of silliness in our lives and the things that bring us joy. Help us to be wise in the ways we admit our foolish mistakes to you. Amen.

SARA BATTS-NEALE

Stubborn hearts

Thus says the Lord: For the sake of your lives, take care that you do not bear a burden on the sabbath day. (v. 21, NRSV)

I don't think our society likes the idea of a sabbath. We're bombarded with ideas about self-care, most of which seem to involve buying or doing something. Just resting isn't productive enough! Yet keeping sabbath is not a minor commandment. It's on the same list as murder, adultery and covetousness. We'd never dream of boasting about how jealous we were, but it's not uncommon to hear people being proud of never taking a break because they're so busy.

As with us, so with the people of Judah. The people had simply stopped keeping the sabbath. It's one of the rules that mark out God's people – with us, too. It is countercultural to keep a sabbath – to switch off, to do no work, and thus allow others the chance to rest too. Throughout Jeremiah's prophecies are the themes of justice and obedience. As we've touched on earlier, there is a school of thought that much of the editing of Jeremiah happened after the exile to explain why the exile happened. The people rejected the covenant, so God rejected them. This extract may be one of the examples of editing – a sermon added after the event addressing one of the most straightforward ways in which the covenant had been broken.

Rest is crucial for our spiritual well-being. Few of us can take a complete break from everything one day a week – but a pattern of rest is helpful for our functioning. When we create space, we give God a chance to act with and in us. It's terribly tempting to steer our own course through a busy life, stopping every now and again in church to allow God a chance to join in. But we're not called to do that – we're called to walk closely with God. Can we take steps towards that today?

'Come to me, all you who are weary and burdened, and I will give you rest. Take my yoke upon me and learn from me, for I am gentle and humble in heart, and you will find rest for your souls' (Matthew 11:28–29, NIV).

SARA BATTS-NEALE

Exiled hearts

Do not let the prophets and the diviners who are among you deceive you, and do not listen to your dreams that you dream. (v. 8, NRSV)

It's likely you've seen or owned something printed with Jeremiah 29:11. It's a widely quoted verse, but I believe it's also often quoted unhelpfully.

The first exiles are now in Babylon. How do they sing the songs of the Lord in this place (Psalm 137)? Jeremiah writes a letter of prophecy. In it, he tells them to settle down and rebuild their lives: plant gardens, marry, have children; seek the welfare of the city you are in, and it will provide your welfare. But there's a catch – it will be 70 years before they're able to return to Jerusalem and in the meantime, there's still more disaster to come there, because there are still false prophets in Jerusalem. So, when we take verse 11 and apply it just to our own personal circumstances, we're losing rather a lot of its context. God's plan is not for personal prosperity or ease for individuals but a restoration of a whole community – and it won't happen yet. I'm not sure I'd be terribly reassured by a prophecy that all will be well but not until 2095!

Moreover, when we take this one line from Jeremiah's letter to an exiled community and apply it to people hurting today, does it suggest we're not really listening to those who share their pain? As a newly single woman in my mid-30s, struggling with debt, relocation and trying to renew my relationship with God, being told God had a plan for me was really not terribly helpful. What I needed then was friends who would take my pain seriously and help me find a way to live. In other words, I needed all of Jeremiah's counsel about how to settle in a strange land – not just a snippet.

Lord God, your word is the light on my path and the lamp for my feet. I am so grateful that there is wisdom for life in all of scripture. Amen.

SARA BATTS-NEALE

Unheeding hearts

'Whether it is favourable or unfavourable, we will obey the Lord our God, to whom we are sending you, so that it will go well with us, for we will obey the Lord our God.' (v. 6, NIV)

I'm not a parent myself, but I gather it's rather frustrating to tell a child explicitly to do something, only to watch them do exactly the opposite. Your instructions might not have been a prophecy from God, but all the same, you'd like to have thought your words and wisdom carried some weight.

Yesterday we were with the exiles in Babylon. Today we are with those left behind. Unsurprisingly, the people are looking for stability and so Jeremiah is approached. Notice how the people – the remnant left behind, still God's people – ask Jeremiah to talk to 'your God' rather than 'our God'. Jeremiah is asked for a prophecy – what should the people do? How do they find security now? They're tempted by the apparent refuge they see over the border in Egypt. The answer from God is clear: stay put, and you'll prosper. Serve the king of Babylon. Don't, whatever you do, go to Egypt. Well, it's not too much of a spoiler to say that the people completely ignore Jeremiah and with disastrous consequences.

Subservience to the king of Babylon was not the answer that the people wanted. They perhaps wanted something dramatic – an obvious sign that all would be well. I wonder if there is any resonance there for your life. Perhaps you would run a mile from the idea of a dramatic change – or maybe you're chafing under the yoke of familiarity and routine. Without a personal Jeremiah to consult, we have to trust that God will show us new opportunities or confirm us in our continuity, learning lessons from those who have stepped out (or stayed home!) ahead of us.

Lord God, we thank you for those who have helped us discern the way forward in our lives and for the guidance we have in prayer, scripture and counsel. Amen.

SARA BATTS-NEALE

Hopeful hearts

They shall all know me, from the least of them to the greatest, says the Lord, for I will forgive their iniquity, and remember their sin no more. (v. 34, NRSV)

This week we have seen how repeated warnings about ignoring the obligations to live justly and to walk in God's ways fell on deaf ears. Wednesday's reading was a clear reminder to live within the law, given to create the identity of God's people. The trouble is that laws have to be learned. They're an outside influence.

One way of thinking about it is like this: some people can sing beautifully before they're even taught; others, me included, can hold a tune but need to follow both written music and accompaniment. Without the external props, I'd struggle to sing without going off-key. God wanted his people to sing his song, and he gave them the law to help keep them in tune. Unfortunately, they thought that just having the sheet music was enough – they could sing whatever tune they wanted, to whichever god they chose, and it wouldn't matter. Those who were still singing God's song – like Jeremiah – would sound wrong, because so many others were doing something different. God wanted it to be different, so effectively he ripped up the sheet music – that's what the exile represented. In the promise of the new covenant, God will give people the ability to sing the song without needing the music. The song will be innate. All the people need to do is look to their hearts.

That's the promise we have in this new covenant. The new covenant we have in Christ is that we're not relying on an external law to keep us as God's people. We do have external props – scripture, to remind us what the kingdom's song sounds like; communities to help strengthen our voice – but ultimately, our relationship with God through Christ teaches us the song of our life with him. Let's go forth and sing.

'I will sing to the Lord all my life; I will sing praise to my God as long as I live' (Psalm 104:33, NIV).

SARA BATTS-NEALE

The Servant Songs and Jesus' fulfilment of the prophecies

Elaine Storkey writes…

Grappling with the prophecies of Isaiah can sometimes be intimidating; Jewish and Christian scholars have been studying them for centuries. In our Bible reflections we're looking at four specific passages of great significance to Christians, which have brought many blessings.

Together the following passages are called the 'Servant Songs' simply because they focus on 'the Lord's servant'. Sometimes we get to know the servant through God's description of him. Sometimes God speaks directly to him, with words of approval. At other times the servant speaks for himself, sharing his heart. In the final song, Isaiah acts as prophetic narrator.

We learn from the voices in these songs (or poems) that God has chosen this servant to 'bring justice to the nations' (Isaiah 42:1, NIV). He is to lead the people of Israel back to God and be a light to people of other nations. His life is marked by obedience, gentleness and perseverance. His task is enormous and costly, yet he sees it through to the end.

Though the servant is honoured by God, he's treated badly by many; the third and fourth songs describe his suffering and humiliation. The fourth song discloses why he undergoes all this. It is to take away the sins and guilt of others, to sacrifice himself for them. Yet, despite discouragement, injustice, ordeals and agony, the servant knows ultimate victory.

Christians have long connected the servant with the Messiah, Jesus, following the witness of the New Testament. In Matthew's gospel, the servant's characteristics (Isaiah 42:1–4) are identified in Jesus (Matthew 12:18–21). In Mark, Jesus discloses himself as the one who came 'to serve, and to give his life as a ransom for many' (Mark 10:45). In Acts, the apostle Philip interprets the fourth song (Isaiah 53:7) to an Ethiopian official, explaining its fulfilment in Jesus (Acts 8:26–35). In Philippians, Paul speaks movingly of Jesus emptying himself, taking the form of a servant (2:7)

The compelling parallels between Isaiah's prophecies and the New Testament accounts of Jesus' suffering and death convince Christians that the Servant Songs speak of him. As we absorb Isaiah's prophetic vision, may our lives be challenged and our hearts filled with gratitude and praise.

God's gentle servant will bring justice

'I will put my Spirit on him, and he will bring justice to the nations. He will not shout or cry out, or raise his voice in the streets. A bruised reed he will not break, and a smouldering wick he will not snuff out.' (vv. 1–3, NIV)

The old British idea of servants is summed up in shows like *Downton Abbey* or films such as *The Remains of the Day*, where everything operates through the class system. Hierarchy among servants mirrors the culture as a whole, and loyalty to the landowning family is the key requirement. P.G. Wodehouse's novels treat class more humorously because the dim upper-class Bertie Wooster constantly needs the wit and wisdom of his intellectually superior butler, Jeeves; but status is always the subtext.

The servant described in this first Servant Song is different. He is God's servant, chosen by God, covered with God's Spirit, and God delights in him. But he is not called to uphold the status of those he serves. Instead, he is called to bring justice on earth, so that even distant islands can put their hope in him. This is a task he will not relinquish, but see through, faithfully, until it is finished.

What marks his servanthood is the way he does that. He's not domineering or self-assertive, drawing attention to his mission. Rather than him enacting justice via threats or success through eradicating failures, Isaiah gives us the lovely image of the servant not snuffing out a smouldering candle or snapping a useless reed. The servant understands our human brokenness. He sees the fragility of those of us who feel defeated and are ready to give up. And he is willing to work patiently and gently with us, until we begin to flourish.

This picture of the servant speaks straight into our hearts, especially those who've endured injustice and know the discouragement of living in an unfair world. Many of us have times when we wonder if anything we do is worthwhile. We can trust the servant to be with us in our struggles and give us confidence to carry on.

Lord, we thank you for your gentleness and steadfast love. Please give us servant hearts so that we may serve other people with sensitivity and patience. Amen.

ELAINE STORKEY

The servant is God's promise for the whole world

'I, the Lord, have called you… I will keep you and will make you to be a covenant for the people and a light for the Gentiles, to open eyes that are blind, to free captives from prison and to release from the dungeon those who sit in darkness.' (vv. 6–7, NIV)

Here, in his supreme power, God speaks directly to his servant about his role in God's purposes. The intimate fatherly image of God holding the servant's hand to keep him safe shows us the closeness between the two of them. The plans God has for Israel are going to be accomplished through the servant. He will not only reaffirm the promises God made to his people, he will himself be God's new covenant with them.

The servant's first mission is to the people of Israel, but then God points far beyond the nation's borders to the rest of the world. The servant is going to bring the Gentiles into the orbit of God's love and salvation. He is going to open eyes that are blind and release people from bondage and darkness. Isaiah repeats these promises in chapter 61, and Jesus reads his words centuries later when he unrolls the scroll in the synagogue (Luke 4:18–19). The Gentiles, who have not known God's love or previously felt included in his promises, will now know that the Lord is their God also.

Christians take it for granted today that the revelation of God's forgiving love is available for all. But this was radical news for the people of Israel, who, as God's chosen ones, failed to recognise that God's welcome was universal. When Jesus read Isaiah's prophecy to fellow Jewish worshippers, every eye in the synagogue was on him (Luke 4:20), and when he declared that the prophecy was fulfilled in their very presence, it must have been a moment of deep revelation and challenge.

I wonder what first led you to believe in Jesus. Whether it was through moments of deep revelation or that you have had faith from infancy, you're part of the fulfilment of this prophecy.

Lord, we praise you that you are the author of creation and God of the entire world. We pray that we will be free from discrimination and narrow sightedness and recognise your calling on people from every nation. Amen.

ELAINE STORKEY

Prophecy is from God

'I am the Lord; that is my name! I will not yield my glory to another or my praise to idols. See, the former things have taken place, and new things I declare; before they spring into being I announce them to you.' (NIV)

Prophecy is not merely a prophet speaking from their own knowledge or insight. It is God's word given for people to hear and absorb. Here Isaiah rounds off the first Servant Song with God's self-identification. God speaking through the prophet is the only God: the creator of the universe and its very life-giver.

Isaiah reminds us often that God will not share his glory and praise with idols because idols are humanly made from something in creation. In Isaiah's day they were ornate statues of wood or stone. In our day they're the multiple expressions of money, sex, power and the self. Yet they are all worshipped in God's place. Our wants, whims, choices, decisions have such prominence in our culture that it seems blasphemous to do something not in our self-interest! Isaiah challenges the futility of praying to gods that cannot save (Isaiah 45:20).

Prophecies from God operate within many different time zones, for God is the author of time. God tells us that some things disclosed through Isaiah have already taken place, but what he says now is yet to happen. In giving the Servant Songs to Isaiah, he is speaking about a far-off future, which Isaiah himself will never experience. Yet, through God's Holy Spirit, Isaiah can prophesy to those yet unborn that Messiah will come as God's servant to endure suffering and pain for our sakes.

Isaiah would not know when his prophecies might be fulfilled. Those living in the centuries following would not know either. But eventually, those who encountered Jesus would know. We can be so grateful for those gospel authors who wrote about the prophecies' fulfilment in Jesus. We can be thankful for Peter's confession, empowered by the Holy Spirit: 'You are the Messiah, the Son of the living God' (Matthew 16:16).

Lord, please make us more aware of those things in our lives which take greater priority than they should. Help us to dethrone all our idols, to know you as God and to serve you with fuller hearts. Amen.

ELAINE STORKEY

The servant named and known from mother's womb

Before I was born the Lord called me; from my mother's womb he has spoken my name. He made my mouth like a sharpened sword, in the shadow of his hand he hid me; he made me into a polished arrow.
(vv. 1–2, NIV)

The servant himself does the narration in this second Servant Song, describing how he grew in secret in his mother's womb, hidden from everyone else, but seen and fashioned by God. I'm struck by the telling metaphors he uses – for example, that God has made his mouth a 'sharpened sword'. We find this same image in Hebrews 4:12, where it's applied to the word of God, which penetrates the soul and spirit and 'judges the thoughts and attitudes of the heart'. Jesus himself is also identified as God's word, in the powerful opening of John's gospel: 'In the beginning was the Word, and the Word was with God, and the Word was God' (1:1). In Isaiah's prophecy that word becomes a 'polished arrow' (v. 2) conveying swiftness and truth, flying direct to the heart and hitting its target.

When God calls the servant 'Israel, in whom I will display my splendour' (v. 3), we may be puzzled, for Isaiah constantly chides Israel for her unfaithfulness and disobedience towards God, and later says the servant will bring Israel back to God. So, the servant cannot simply be Israel. We must remember this is prophecy. Matthew's gospel interprets Isaiah as prophetically pointing to the new Israel, Jesus (e.g. 2:15; 12:20), the gentle, obedient, faithful servant, who will reveal God's glory to the world.

Throughout the ages people have wanted to see God's divine power. Idols made from gold and precious stones are human statements of what gods must look like. Jesus' own disciples asked him to show them God the Father. We treasure his reply: 'Anyone who has seen me has seen the Father' (John 14:9). Jesus is not only God's unique servant and God's incarnate Word. He is also God's beloved Son.

Lord, we thank you that we hear your word through Jesus and the Holy Spirit, through the scriptures and through creation itself. Help us to understand better the truths of your word and carry them to our generation. Amen.

ELAINE STORKEY

The servant lifted from discouragement

But I said, 'I have laboured in vain; I have spent my strength for nothing at all. Yet what is due to me is in the Lord's hand, and my reward is with my God.' (v. 4, NIV)

This part of the second Servant Song is short but moving. For any of us who struggle with discouragement it is a comfort. The servant shares his disappointment at the little he has achieved. It has cost him dearly, taken so much energy and effort. He's given his all, thrown himself into fulfilling his calling to communicate God's truth to people, but at this moment he feels there is nothing to show for it.

How many times in our lives do we feel the same? Sometimes, the path we have taken on our journey with God has seemed clear. But then, things go wrong, people let us down, decisions turn out badly. It is not uncommon for faithful Christians to question whether their efforts have been a waste of time. Sadly, doubt surfaces at some time in the lives of most of us. Yet the knowledge that God's servant experiences this too can help us put it into perspective.

Why was the servant discouraged? Probably for reasons we will never experience. The passage links it with his calling to bring Israel back to enjoy a renewed relationship with God. So many in Israel did receive his message with joy and repented, but many others rejected the servant and went their own way, despite all the evidence that God was with him.

The fact that the servant can see beyond the disappointment and trust everything to God's hand speaks into any sense of futility we might sometimes have. Despite what he feels, he recognises that God values his faithfulness and commitment, and he knows what is due to him. His discouragement ends with acceptance that God has always been his strength. In those difficult times in life, may we find the same.

Let's hold on to God's response to Paul's discouragement: 'My grace is sufficient for you, for my power is made perfect in weakness' (2 Corinthians 12:9). When we are down, let's lean on God's strength and love.

ELAINE STORKEY

The servant: a light to the nations

'It is too small a thing for you to be my servant to restore the tribes of Jacob… I will also make you a light for the Gentiles, that my salvation may reach to the ends of the earth… Kings will see you and stand up.' (NIV)

God's words to the servant here had huge implications. The servant had been given the job of restoring Israel to God. (This again makes it hard to identify the servant as Israel.) But God repeats his promise that the bigger job will be to reach out to the rest of the world. The Gentile nations are to be brought into God's light. The servant himself is that light; it is through him that salvation may reach to the ends of the world.

What Isaiah sees here is that the breathtaking vision of the kingdom of God extends far beyond the nation of Israel. Its citizens would include people of every race, for God 'the Redeemer and Holy One of Israel' (v. 7) is the God of the entire world. Kings and princes across the globe will recognise that and honour the servant rejected by his own people. They will know his identity as God's chosen one and pay homage.

Today more than 2.3 billion people, from every continent, identify as believers in Jesus: a third of the world's population. Though belief is declining in Europe, the gospel has spread rapidly in Africa and Asia. Down through the centuries world rulers have confessed faith in Christ, like our own late Queen Elizabeth II. In a Christmas broadcast she said: 'God sent into the world a unique person… a Saviour with the power to forgive.' It was a witness shared by other monarchs too.

Yet Isaiah's prophecy is not yet completely fulfilled. Against secular and religious opposition, we must continue to pray and proclaim the good news of Christ until God's salvation does reach the ends of the earth. And we must remind leaders and rulers everywhere that the servant principle is the only principle on which just and peaceful governments can be built.

Lord, we pray into the turmoil of our world, where wars devastate and conflict dominates. We pray that you will raise up leaders with integrity who seek peace and justice and open the path to faith in you. Amen.

ELAINE STORKEY

As the servant learns, he teaches

The Sovereign Lord has given me a well-instructed tongue, to know the word that sustains the weary. He wakens me morning by morning, wakens my ear to listen like one being instructed. The Sovereign Lord has opened my ears; I have not been rebellious, I have not turned away. (NIV)

In this third Servant Song, the servant introduces himself as a learner-teacher. He receives his 'well-instructed tongue' from God and listens from the moment he wakes so that he can teach with discernment and empathy. We find no sense of self-importance or superiority in this servant-teacher, only a desire to serve God and communicate wisdom to others.

I find this a challenge to our present age. Bombarded by prolific communication, people often respond quickly and superficially to what they hear. Studies show that concentration spans have shrunk and people expect immediate access to information, so spend less time learning and reflecting. Because social media expands access to people we don't know, digital platforms like X often carry banal and uninformed reactions or offensive put-downs of the views of others.

The servant, in contrast, listens and learns before he speaks and treats people with respect. He understands those who are vulnerable. His example reinforces the maxim that no one should become a teacher without first having been a learner. This applies to leadership in any walk of life, including the church. Jesus' disciples were learners long before they were apostolic leaders. Jesus often had to correct their understanding, not least about status and service (for example, Mark 10:42–44).

When Christian leaders are not committed to learning humbly and prayerfully from God, they expose the church to danger. A teacher's own opinions can become absolute, their lifestyles closed to rebuke. The only safeguard against heresy and falsehood is the humility of learning before God. We need 'instructed', not 'unbridled', tongues (James 3:3), trained patiently by God to speak peace to conflict and truth to power.

Pray for the teachers and pastors in your church, that they will remain faithful to their calling. Pray too that God will raise up humble leaders and protect them from falsehoods and delusions that would lead them astray.

ELAINE STORKEY

The servant accepts humiliation and abuse

I offered my back to those who beat me, my cheeks to those who pulled out my beard; I did not hide my face from mocking and spitting… I have set my face like flint, and I know I will not be put to shame. (NIV)

The servant offers a stark picture of his abuse and humiliation. It's like an uncontrolled gang, physically and emotionally bullying a defenceless individual. We shudder at the image of hair being pulled out; the shame and indignity of being spat at makes us recoil. God's servant identifies here with many who have experienced degradation at the hands of a mob.

Yet the servant isn't simply a passive victim. Notice that he says he 'offered' his back and his face to his abusers. Even though he is being attacked and violated, he is not allowing the oppressors to dictate the terms or his own reactions. He permits them to harm him. He doesn't fight back or allow resentment and bitterness to build up.

These, in themselves, are lessons for us. In the face of hatred most people seek revenge, often to the extent of it dominating their lives. Victims can end up mimicking the behaviour of those who oppressed them; it's common to hate back. But violence dehumanises the inflictor and can turn victims into mirror images of those who've harmed them. Seeking justice is important, but prolonged bitterness brings more harm than release.

However, this prophecy is about more than physical abuse. It is a prophecy of Israel's rejection of God's servant; a prophecy the New Testament identifies with Jesus. In Matthew's gospel, at the end of a phoney trial before High Priest Caiaphas, we're told they spat in his face and struck him with their fists. Others slapped him and said, 'Prophesy to us, Messiah. Who hit you?' (Matthew 26:67–68). Isaiah's prophecy also anticipates Jesus' resolve and persistent trust that God will grant justice: 'I have set my face like flint, and I know I will not be put to shame.'

Lord, thank you for willingly enduring hostility and hatred for our sakes. Please help us to learn how to respond to those who would harm us and how to help others who are victimised. And keep us from bitterness. Amen.

ELAINE STORKEY

119

God knows the servant's innocence

He who vindicates me is near. Who then will bring charges against me? Let us face each other! Who is my accuser? Let him confront me! It is the Sovereign Lord who helps me. (vv. 8–9, NIV)

Many years ago, my husband used to take his students to observe court proceedings. They once heard an irate senior judge call the prosecution's case 'poppycock' and indignantly throw it out for lack of evidence. Here, the servant expresses indignance that this trial should be taking place. Yet he has confidence in the outcome. Two factors explain this.

The first is that God is near and will vindicate him. He knows God has been watching as he allows himself to be persecuted and falsely accused. He believes the scripture that 'the Lord will vindicate his people, have compassion on his servants' (Deuteronomy 32:36, NRSV). God is near in another sense too. The servant has an intimate relationship with him. God knows his heart; he's been chosen to fulfil God's purpose for the world. So, it's not for the servant to try to sort things out or plead his own case. He just needs to trust. His manner and attitude express what the apostle Paul would later tell the church in Rome: 'If God is for us, who can be against us?' (Romans 8:31).

The second factor is that no one will be able to bring any evidence of wrongdoing against him. His real accusers do not even come out themselves to confront him. They have nothing but lies to offer and will eventually be put to shame themselves. Like a moth-eaten garment, they will ultimately disintegrate into nothing.

I find the parallels between Isaiah's prophecy and the court process which faced Jesus very powerful. The details match. False witnesses, pretence, hypocrisy and trumped-up charges all combined to find Jesus guilty of blasphemy. Isaiah's words from the servant identified the corruption hundreds of years earlier. Yet though injustice happened, Jesus, the servant, was vindicated. Ultimate victory belonged to Jesus.

Lord, we're conscious today of many people across the world facing injustice, incarcerated or undergoing torture for their faith in Jesus. We pray for them and for those who make their plight known. Amen.

ELAINE STORKEY

The servant will be raised up and prosper

See, my servant will act wisely; he will be raised and lifted up and highly exalted… so he will sprinkle many nations, and kings will shut their mouths because of him. For what they were not told, they will see, and what they have not heard, they will understand. (vv. 13, 15, NIV)

I was puzzled at first why the fourth Servant Song seemed to begin at the end of the servant's story. For Isaiah starts with the voice of God sounding a triumphant note of victory. Yet after re-reading the rest of the song in chapter 53, it was a relief to hear these three verses first. Isaiah was giving us some assurance of hope, some achievement of end purpose before his prophecy went into the suffering and disfigurement of the servant (v. 14).

God reminds us of how people will acknowledge the servant's wisdom. The words 'raised', 'lifted up' and 'highly exalted' all carry the same meaning. The servant is to be publicly celebrated for who he really is. This anticipates the gospel of John, where it says: 'Just as Moses lifted up the snake in the wilderness, so the Son of Man must be lifted up, that everyone who believes may have eternal life in him' (3:14–15). God prophetically assures us that his purposes will be fulfilled; the servant will prosper in his redemptive work.

Notice the impact of the servant's work, especially on those beyond the nation of Israel. They will be 'sprinkled' – a reference to the ritual cleansing from sin we find in Leviticus 4:6. Their rulers will be astonished, even speechless. For they will see and hear for themselves what they never knew before, as God's revelation reaches beyond the borders of Israel to every nation. Once again, Isaiah stresses this truth in his Servant Song. Gentiles, right down the ages, will be included in the divine redemption plan. We know this has happened and rejoice that God has reached out even to us, with forgiveness, grace and love.

Lord, we want to exalt your name and truth in our own lives and witness. Please give us boldness and reveal to us how we can be more effective in making you known. Amen.

ELAINE STORKEY

Insignificance hides the servant's value

He had no beauty or majesty to attract us to him, nothing in his appearance that we should desire him. He was despised and rejected by mankind, a man of suffering, and familiar with pain. Like one from whom men hide their faces he was despised, and we held him in low esteem. (vv. 2–3, NIV)

Isaiah himself takes on the narration in this fourth Servant Song and tells us about the servant's background. In human terms he comes from nowhere – he is a 'root out of dry ground' (v. 2). And in terms of status, he is nothing – he comes with no glamour, no pomp, no royal identity, no finery or affluence. Isaiah hints again at his marred appearance: people can't bear to look at him. Most onlookers considered him of no significance.

Added to that we learn of his emotions. Older translations say he was 'a man of sorrows, and acquainted with grief' (KJV). Those words imply disease and illness, but also affliction and calamity – being overwhelmed by terrible circumstances. Isaiah is stressing again why people hid their faces from him – they didn't want to engage with his suffering.

This is not unusual in our own day. Many people faint at seeing blood ooze from a vein. We shudder at screen images of mangled human bodies in the carnage of war. Only psychopathic people enjoy the pain of others. For the rest of us it's profoundly disturbing and we don't want to be onlookers. Even being with someone in great emotional or mental distress can be a challenge. It's easy to feel quickly out of our depth and run from involvement in others' torment.

Isaiah's picture of the servant's ordeals immediately draws us to Jesus. As Jesus hung on the cross, subject to much suffering, many must have looked away from his tortured body. Yet some would have hidden their faces from him for another reason – guilt. They recognised the hypocrisy, injustice and evil he bore, and they knew that they were implicated. At the deepest spiritual level, we know we are too. For human sin is an ongoing problem for us all. We thank God for Jesus.

Who do you know who needs your prayers and practical support right now because of spiritual problems or suffering? Why not pray for them and ask God to give them peace and hope.

ELAINE STORKEY

The purpose of the servant's suffering

Surely he took up our pain and bore our suffering, yet we considered him punished by God, stricken by him, and afflicted. But he was pierced for our transgressions, he was crushed for our iniquities; the punishment that brought us peace was on him, and by his wounds we are healed. (vv. 4–5, NIV)

These verses unfold the heart of the servant's purpose, mission and his identification with us, and offer a powerful link between the Old Testament and the gospel. I love the way Isaiah begins with 'surely'. He's saying that, despite our wrong assumptions, the servant's suffering was caused by us.

What were those wrong assumptions? It was often supposed that people brought suffering on themselves, that God afflicted them because of their wrongdoing (see for example John 9:1–2). Isaiah makes it very clear that what the servant endured was because of *our* wrongdoing. He suffered on our behalf and was punished instead of us. Notice the way the 'we' here includes Isaiah! He doesn't point the finger at others but accepts that he's also complicit in the world's sin. It's stressed again when he says: 'We all, like sheep, have gone astray' and 'the Lord has laid on him the iniquity of us all' (v. 6). No one is innocent. Human sin is ubiquitous.

Isaiah identifies two important aspects of the servant's mission which come together: his ministry of healing, and his ministry of forgiveness. Isaiah refers to healing – 'He took up our pain' – then to atonement – 'The punishment that brought us peace was on him.' (Priests' hands 'put' people's sin on sacrificial animals.) In Isaiah's prophecy the servant is both wounded healer and willing scapegoat for sin. His wounds heal us and take our penalty.

All these words link the prophecy to the gospels. Even the word 'pierced' takes us to the piercing of Jesus' side on the cross (John 19:34). The early apostles knew that these songs in Isaiah pointed directly to Jesus (Acts 3:18; 1 Peter 2:24–25). As Good Friday approaches, we're thankful too for this vision of Christ, and even more for his sacrificial love.

Lord, we thank you that the apostles and the early church saw the fulfilment of the Servant Songs in Jesus. We pray for those of the Jewish faith today, that many of them will receive this revelation. Amen.

ELAINE STORKEY

The servant understood by those who seek truth

He was oppressed and afflicted, yet he did not open his mouth; he was led like a lamb to the slaughter… By oppression and judgement he was taken away. Yet who of his generation protested?… He was assigned a grave with the wicked, and with the rich in his death. (NIV)

Seven hundred years after Isaiah's prophecy, this passage turns up in the scriptures again. It's in the exciting story of the Ethiopian court official, where the Holy Spirit transported the apostle Philip to explain to him what the passage meant (Acts 8:26–39). We shouldn't be surprised at that, for it was the same Holy Spirit who revealed the prophecy to Isaiah.

I suspect the Ethiopian had lots of questions. He would have known the reference to the sacrificial lamb, but probably didn't understand why the lamb's silence was significant. What kind of humiliation or injustice did this person suffer, and why was he cut off without descendants? For Philip, the answers were easy. He fervently believed that Isaiah was prophesying about Jesus; that all the references to silence, oppression and injustice were a commentary on Jesus being subjected to a makeshift trial and wrongly convicted. He knew too that Jesus was utterly innocent and that what he went through was on behalf of others.

The precision of his death and burial must also have startled Philip's seeker. To be executed as a criminal but given a rich man's grave was not a normal process at any time. Yet the description envisaged so long ago perfectly fitted Jesus.

I'm so glad this Servant Song was carried forward into the experience of the early church as they communicated to others what it cost Jesus to die for our sins. It's thrilling to see the power of the Holy Spirit in taking Isaiah's prophecy into the hearts and minds of those seeking truth. Let's pray for all who seek God, and let's give thanks that Jesus died for us and that, like Philip and the Ethiopian, we can trust him completely.

Lord, we worship you for your atoning love. We praise you that on this Good Friday we can take time to remember Jesus' death on the cross and give thanks from our hearts for his triumph over evil. Amen.

ELAINE STORKEY

The servant is vindicated by God

Though the Lord makes his life an offering for sin, he will see his offspring and prolong his days, and the will of the Lord will prosper in his hand. After he has suffered, he will see the light of life and be satisfied… I will give him a portion among the great. (NIV)

Today we are in the day between Christ's death and resurrection. We think of those grieving women who watched Jesus die, now preparing the oils and spices to anoint his body in the tomb when sabbath has passed. We see their anxiety as they ponder how to remove the heavy gravestone and accomplish their task.

Thankfully, we know what they didn't, for we have the gospel account of the 'third day'. We also have the finale of the Servant Songs, in which Isaiah foresees the ultimate victory of the servant. Though the servant gave his life as a 'guilt offering' for our sins, dying in our place, that was not to be the end of the story.

God's promises for the servant abound. He will 'see his offspring', 'prolong his days' and 'see the light of life and be satisfied' (vv. 10–11). Jesus, God's servant and Son, knows his work of atonement is finished, as he proclaimed from the cross. He will live in victory as he rises from the tomb. His days will be prolonged as he ministers and commissions his disciples. His offspring through the centuries will be too numerous to count.

The women huddled together in grief would be first witnesses of the truth of Isaiah's prophecy. We thank God that we see more. We see Jesus, the servant, as the centrepiece of the New Testament. We hear his words to his disciples that he's been given all authority in heaven and on earth (Matthew 28:18). We read that his name is above every name and that every knee shall bow to him (Philippians 2:9–11; Revelation 19:16). We know his reign will be over the entire earth and that his kingdom will be forever (Hebrews 1:8). We wait in anticipation for the day of resurrection.

Lord, thank you for your faithful prophet, Isaiah, and for revealing to him your purposes in the redemption of humankind through Jesus. May our lives be centred on your love. Amen.

ELAINE STORKEY

Jesus is risen!

Jackie Harris writes…

We've spent the last two weeks looking at how Jesus fulfilled the ancient prophecies of Isaiah about a servant sent by God to bring his people back to him. We've thought about some of the things Jesus said and did and the manner of his death, which parallel Isaiah's vision of the servant. That vision included the promise of resurrection, and so, as we move on to Easter Day, we're going to look at the experiences of Jesus' disciples and others in the days following Jesus' crucifixion.

We begin on that first morning, imagining what it must have been like for those women who were first to hear the amazing news that Jesus was alive. Then we look at different people's experiences of meeting or seeing the resurrected Jesus. We'll meet those who are feeling lost or fearful, those struggling to make sense of things or struggling to believe, those who have retreated behind locked doors or are seeking refuge in the familiar. Some don't want to believe Jesus is alive, others take time to believe; but for everyone who encounters the risen Lord, life will never be the same again.

How are you approaching this Easter Day? Perhaps you too are feeling fearful or lost, are seeking refuge, or are struggling to believe. Maybe you're feeling nothing at all. Sometimes, if we have been Christians a long time, we can become blasé about things. It's all very familiar. 'We know all that', we think.

Let's take a moment to dwell on the amazing truth that Jesus was crucified, died and was buried, then rose again from the dead. This is life changing. Let's remember that he appeared to hundreds of people and did far more than we have recorded in the gospels.

John makes clear that he couldn't record everything Jesus said and did (John 20:30; 21:25), but that what is written is set down so that we 'may believe that Jesus is the Messiah, the Son of God, and that by believing [we] may have life in his name' (John 20:31, NIV).

As we read about the risen Jesus, may we be willing to bring to him our doubts, confusion, fears or emptiness, and receive again his assurance that he is risen and that he is with us now and forever. Hallelujah!

The women at the tomb

On the first day of the week, very early in the morning, the women took the spices they had prepared and went to the tomb… but the men said to them, 'Why do you look for the living among the dead? He is not here; he has risen!' (vv. 1, 5–6, NIV)

Have you been to an outdoors Easter morning sunrise service? It is one of my favourite occasions, whether it is held in a wood, on a hillside or on the beach. As the familiar, spine-tingling story of that first Easter morning is told, I so relate to those brave, caring women as they made their way to the burial tomb of Jesus. I too have got up in the dark to go to Jesus; I too have been preparing myself, albeit rather differently, but with expectation.

Let's picture ourselves among these women, quietly hurrying through the coming dawn, careful not to draw attention, yet determined to do right by Jesus in anointing his dead body with appropriate spices as a last act of love. Imagine seeing the stone out of place and the empty tomb, the distress, the questions and the sudden appearance of angelic beings. What must it have been like to be the first to hear the news that was to shake the foundations of human existence and to be honoured as women to take this treasure back to the doubting male disciples.

Consider how it felt to be trusted with earth-shattering truth, in a society that regarded women as mere possessions and second-rate citizens; to remember those two remarkable women, Mary and Elizabeth, who had similarly been the first to respond in faith to the angel Gabriel over 30 years previously.

See yourself among these women: overwhelmed with incredulous joy, hardly daring to breathe, hardly daring to believe, knowing this was going to change the world; laughing, exclaiming, wide-eyed with wonder, holding on to each other in joy; our deepest, tenderest hopes about Jesus beginning to be realised; saying to each other: 'I knew it. I knew Jesus was like this. I knew he could not be beaten. I knew he was this good.'

Read Isaiah 54:5. You are his, and he is yours.

DI ARCHER

Forever changed

Jesus said to her, 'Mary.' She turned towards him and cried out in Aramaic, 'Rabboni!' (which means 'Teacher'). (v. 16, NIV)

Jesus had transformed Mary's life before. He'd rid her of demons and healed her. He'd called her to follow him, and she'd willingly accepted. She'd walked beside him as he did what could only be described as miraculous. She believed he was who he said he was, and she was forever grateful for that first encounter she had with him, a moment which changed everything.

This moment here in the garden transformed Mary's life too, and again it was Jesus who was responsible for it. Only this time, he was gone. She sobbed as she tried to make sense of how she would ever go on without him. The time without him she'd known prior to this was only riddled with demons and darkness. She could never go back, of course, but how could she go forward without him, she wondered.

Here in the garden, with nothing more than a word, she knew she was speaking to the Lord. Her Lord. The familiarity with which Jesus called her name was all that Mary needed to know that this was him. But how? And now what?

We see in verse 17 that she held on to him. Of course she did. For without holding on, how was she to know that he wouldn't leave again? And yet when Jesus told her to let go, she obeyed. Although she knew that it might mean she'd never see him again, she let go and let God's will be done. Her life was forever changed, just like ours is, all because of a man named Jesus.

Lord God, thank you for sending your Son. Thank you that you know us wholly and completely like you did Mary. Thank you for sending your Holy Spirit so that through him we know that you will never leave nor forsake us. Amen.

NAOMI AIDOO

A story silenced

'You are to say, "His disciples came during the night and stole him away while we were asleep."' (v. 13, NIV)

I remember hearing a documentary a few years ago featuring some of the women who'd worked on the code-breaking operations at Bletchley Park during World War II. I was impressed by their work and the vital role it had in bringing the war to an end, but I think what astonished me most was the way they'd kept the secrets of their life in that place, some of them only telling their stories for the first time when they were in their 90s. I wondered what impact such secrecy had had on them.

Today's reading introduces us to another group of people who had to keep their story silent. Perhaps we have less sympathy for a bunch of guards who signed the first-century equivalent of a non-disclosure agreement and got a massive pay-out in return, but the effect was still the same. They experienced something monumental which they were unable to share. The earlier part of this passage tells us that they fainted at the sight of the angel who moved the stone, but when they went to the chief priests, they were able to tell them 'everything that had happened' (v. 11), so we can safely assume they came round fairly quickly and saw the women, the opened tomb and maybe even Jesus. What must it have been like to hold such a life-changing experience inside for fear of punishment, even death?

I don't know about you, but my reasons for keeping quiet are much less impressive than that. I keep quiet out of embarrassment, either fear of sounding mad or a desire not to make someone else feel awkward. Yet when I tell the story of my most significant encounters with God, I find deep blessing, as does the person I'm telling.

Jesus, we pray for those who dare not tell of their encounters with you for fear of losing everything. Comfort them in the face of persecution and help them know exactly when to speak and when to stay silent. Amen.

LYNDALL BYWATER

Expecting the unexpected

He asked them, 'What are you discussing together as you walk along?' They stood still, their faces downcast. One of them, named Cleopas, asked him, 'Are you the only one visiting Jerusalem who does not know the things that have happened there in these days?' (vv. 17–18, NIV)

A number of years ago, on a whistle-stop tour of Israel, I was on a minibus exiting Jerusalem. I looked out of the window as it started to rain and was surprised to see a small sign which said 'Emmaus Road' and an arrow pointing west.

The day Cleopas and his companion set out to walk some seven miles home to an obscure town, not mentioned anywhere else in the Bible, might have been just such another seemingly normal, rather gloomy day. They were shocked and upset, and the last thing they would have expected was to meet the risen Christ.

I think we all find it difficult to believe that Jesus will speak to us or act in the middle of something mundane, particularly when things haven't been going well. I confess I don't expect him to be present on a dark morning when we are trying to get the kids to school!

Some scholars think that the unnamed companion to Cleopas was actually Mary, the wife of Clopas, who is mentioned as being at the foot of the cross (John 19:25). If this is the case, then Mary would have been carrying significant trauma from the events she had witnessed. Again, feeling depressed can lower our expectation of hearing God speak.

However, as the couple walking to Emmaus discovered, there is no barrier to when or how Jesus can speak to us. He can reveal something of himself to us through a song, a friend, a sermon or a message on social media. But this story reminds us that we need also to ask him, as the couple do at the end of this story, into the things that worry us, the relationships that matter to us and perhaps, most importantly, into our homes and lives.

Father God, teach us to see you when we least expect it and be prepared to be purposeful in inviting you in. Amen.

LIZ HOGARTH

The locked room

On the evening of that first day of the week, when the disciples were together, with the doors locked for fear of the Jewish leaders, Jesus came and stood among them and said, 'Peace be with you!' (v. 19, NIV)

In novels, plays and films, the 'locked room' is a popular and intriguing device. A strange event, usually a crime, has happened in a single location with a limited cast in seemingly impossible circumstances, and we are invited to solve the mystery. Page by page, scene by scene, we keep watching and reading, knowing there will be an answer to the puzzle and ready to congratulate the writer for their ingenuity.

But how is it for the disciples in their locked room? They have retreated here as a place of safety, bewildered by recent events. Their Saviour has been put to death, and they fear the Jewish authorities will be coming for them next. They're terrified by what's happening outside and know that at any moment the door can be broken down.

Then they are joined by another person. The door is locked, so how can this be? What's more, he looks like Jesus, who they know is dead, but this person is as real as they are. He shows them his hands and his feet, and he greets them with peace, offering them consolation in circumstances which seem all-consuming. Confronted by the reality of the risen Lord, they are amazed and filled with joy. He commissions them to continue his work with an anointing of the Holy Spirit.

This locked room offers us so much more than the answer to a riddle. While we wonder at the power and inventiveness of our amazing God, the author of everything, we also see how we are equipped to live and serve the Lord in all circumstances. No matter how overwhelming our troubles, Jesus is always with us, offering peace and courage, getting alongside us so we are never alone. And like him, through the Holy Spirit, we can overcome and share the good news with all the world.

Lord, thank you that you are with me in all circumstances, offering peace, forgiveness and strength. Fill me anew today, that I might be ready to share this good news. Amen.

CATHERINE LARNER

131

Doubt is not the unforgivable sin

'Reach out your hand and put it into my side. Stop doubting and believe.' Thomas said to him, 'My Lord and my God!' Then Jesus told him, 'Because you have seen me, you have believed; blessed are those who have not seen and yet have believed.' (v. 27–29, NIV)

Having once – *once* – licked my plate clean after a delicious dessert, I have been typecast at home as a plate-licker. Sometimes, poor reputations can arise from the simplest of misdemeanours, and this applies to Thomas, who even makes it into the dictionary: 'A doubting Thomas: a person who is sceptical and refuses to believe something without proof.' Let's examine if this is fair.

Verses 19–23 describe the risen Jesus appearing to the disciples as they met in secret, terrified of Jewish retaliation. Thomas wasn't with them. In fleeing from the crucifixion scene, confused and grief-stricken, had he continued to run? The disciples' report of this highly improbable visit led him to declare that he wouldn't – couldn't – believe a word of it unless he saw and touched Jesus' wounds.

I have sometimes sensed that God has read my diary, speaking to me in words I recognise as my own. We have this here. Without Thomas having to repeat his assertion, Jesus invites him into the very encounter he craved. Note what is missing here: a total lack of reprimand. In other gospel stories, the disciples are chastened for their lack of faith; but I think the key difference here is that Thomas – who must have loved Jesus – simply needed the comfort of reassurance.

Finally, all doubt removed, Thomas could see Jesus for who he was: Yahweh, the great I AM. I'm sure his life was changed forever that day.

Have you thought of doubt as the unforgivable sin? Perhaps your questions have put a barrier between you and God. Offer them to him now, asking him for the reassurance you need; then receive his peace.

JANE WALTERS

The breakfast meeting

Simon Peter, Thomas… Nathanael from Cana in Galilee, the sons of Zebedee, and two other disciples were together. 'I'm going out to fish,' Simon Peter told them, and they said, 'We'll go with you.' (vv. 2–3, NIV)

I sometimes forget that the disciples had seen Jesus at least twice already before this breakfast meeting. We've been reading about them over the last two days – the occasion when they were hiding in fear in a locked room (20:19–23) and then again when they gathered in a house and Thomas was with them (20:24–29). So they had spoken with Jesus and rejoiced together, but these were brief meetings and the future remained unclear. Led by Peter, a few of the disciples decide to go fishing, perhaps seeking refuge in doing something that was familiar and reassuring.

However, it's a long and frustrating night until an apparent stranger offers some advice and suggests a different approach. Suddenly their nets are full, and they recognise Jesus. When they reach the shore, they find Jesus cooking breakfast for them. I wonder how many times they had eaten similar meals together during the three years they had spent with him. When he gave them the bread and fish (v. 13), perhaps they remembered another picnic when five small loaves and two fish fed over 5,000 people (6:1–13).

I'm so glad John records this meeting with Jesus. It speaks so much of Jesus' kindness. He meets his disciples in a familiar place and, for Peter especially, there are reminders of their first meeting. Peter had been struggling to catch fish then too (Luke 5:1–11). We will be thinking more about Peter tomorrow, but for now, imagine this group of disciples simply enjoying breakfast and being with Jesus.

Read through the story again. What detail catches your eye? Can you identify with the disciples returning to something familiar? What do you need Jesus to do for you today?

Lord Jesus, you promise to be with us always. Please help me to recognise you with me now. Amen.

JACKIE HARRIS

Declaring my love for Jesus Christ

'Yes, Lord,' [Simon Peter] said, 'you know that I love you.' (v. 15, NIV)

I've had the privilege to visit the Church of the Primacy of Saint Peter. My precious memory is of cool feet in the Sea of Galilee and hot tears streaming down my face. In that moment I felt nothing else mattered but to also declare my love for Jesus, not just three times, but over and over again. Even during such an emotional experience, I took snatches of video.

In writing this note for today, I reflected on the contrast between this easy way to record for posterity and the gospels, which give us only the edited highlights of three years of Jesus' ministry. There were many other things that Jesus did – far too many to record. One that was preserved was the restoration of the relationship with Peter. Peter hasn't really known what to do with himself since his fierce denials of Christ at the crucifixion. Today, he comes face to face with Jesus again.

'Do you love me?' asks Jesus. Impetuous as ever, Peter jumps in straight away. 'You know I do', he says. Then Jesus asks him twice more – three times Peter says he loves Jesus. Three assertions of love made in bright daylight to parallel the three denials on that long dark night before the crucifixion. I wonder why Peter was hurt at the repetition. Afraid, perhaps, that Jesus would never acknowledge, never forgive. Love is an active verb, seen in the actions of others and is lost in empty words. Peter is told to show active love by the command to 'feed my lambs'. Peter, the rock, impetuous, one who inspires all of us who keep getting it wrong, is shown how to love. Peter, like us, is transformed by an encounter with the post-resurrection Jesus. May we declare our love for Jesus today.

'Although you have not seen him, you love him; and even though you do not see him now, you believe in him and rejoice with an indescribable and glorious joy' (1 Peter 1:8, NRSV).

SARA BATTS-NEALE

Jesus' ongoing masterclass

'All authority in heaven and on earth has been given to me. Therefore go and make disciples of all nations… And surely I am with you always, to the very end of the age.' (vv. 18–20, NIV)

My primary school headteacher was witty but terrifying, and he taught a small maths class to advanced learners. Ten-year-old me felt scared about having maths lessons with him. In class, however, we discovered something thrilling – he didn't just lecture maths from the front, he came alongside us and did the tasks with us, like a masterclass. It was more like having a coach than an instructor, and it's the only time I can say that maths felt like fun.

When we hear 'the great commission' read out in church, it can often sound like an intimidating, impossible task: 'Go and make disciples!' But it's meant to feel like an exciting invitation to be part of Jesus' masterclass, working alongside him. I imagine the disciples seeing Jesus resurrected and hearing that incredible proclamation: 'All authority in heaven and on earth has been given to me' (v. 18). Jesus revealed himself as exonerated by God but also divine. The great surprise is that Jesus' 'Therefore…' isn't a proclamation of what he will do to the world, alone, but an invitation to what we will do, working with him. God is not a lecturer but a team worker. There were two responses – doubt and worship (v. 17). It's a reminder that when it comes to Jesus, the opposite of doubt is not belief, but worship. He is worthy.

Making 'disciples of all nations' (v. 19) is only ever done under Jesus' authority and with his presence. There is great comfort and gentleness in that. Think through the elements of these verses: worshipping rather than doubting; making disciples; reaching all nations; teaching people Jesus' instructions; baptising people into Trinitarian Christianity. Which of those elements is God especially prompting you to this week? What can you do to get started?

Dear Jesus, thank you for that comforting promise that you are always with us, 'to the very end of the age' (v. 20). Please give us opportunities to fulfil that great commission in a way that fits us. Amen.

TANYA MARLOW

Jesus' ascension

'You will receive power when the Holy Spirit comes on you; and you will be my witnesses in Jerusalem, and in all Judea and Samaria, and to the ends of the earth.' After he said this, he was taken up before their very eyes, and a cloud hid him from their sight. (vv. 8-9, NIV)

The account of Jesus' ascension gets dismissed by people who point to pre-scientific assumptions about 'heaven' being beyond the sky. But quibbling over heaven's location misses the point. Jesus' words to Mary Magdalene after the resurrection were fulfilled: 'I am ascending to my Father and your Father, to my God and your God' (John 20:17). The disciples' experience recorded by Luke in both accounts was simple: one moment Jesus was with them, the next he was not.

The ascension signalled to the disciples that Jesus' time on earth was finished. In his life, death and resurrection he'd done everything agreed between him and the Father. But this didn't mean his spiritual presence with them had ended, for he had promised his disciples that he'd be present always to the end of the age (Matthew 28:20). Through the ascension, Jesus could become more present than before. He was no longer confined to the limitations of a body, even a resurrected body. Rather than being restrained to one place at one time, he could be everywhere, with the Holy Spirit making his presence known and felt.

The ascension was a turning point for the disciples. They would now become Christ's body more fully. After receiving the Holy Spirit's power at Pentecost, they would experience the authority and gifts to continue the ministry Jesus had begun. They would be built up together. Christ's body would love, heal, teach and proclaim the good news of his salvation to the whole world.

Today, we too are post-ascension followers of Jesus and part of his body on earth. Jesus tells us too that we'll do works he did, and even more, because he's with the Father (John 14:12). If this seems unlikely, perhaps it's time to pray for greater power from the Holy Spirit!

Lord, we thank you that you are with us always. Please give us greater confidence that we can do the work of your body on earth. We pray now for the power of your Holy Spirit. Amen.

ELAINE STORKEY

Matthias, the twelfth apostle

They nominated two men: Joseph… and Matthias. Then they prayed, 'Lord, you know everyone's heart. Show us which of these two you have chosen to take over this apostolic ministry'… Then they cast lots, and the lot fell to Matthias; so he was added to the eleven apostles. (vv. 23–26, NIV)

We don't know about Matthias' personal encounters with Jesus. Indeed, everything we know about Matthias is in these few verses. He wasn't in Jesus' inner circle, but he met the requirements Peter laid out for a replacement for Judas (vv. 11–12), so we know he was among the disciples who had followed Jesus from his baptism. He would have witnessed Jesus' miracles and teaching and may have been among the 72 appointed by Jesus to go ahead of him into the towns and villages (Luke 10:1).

We can assume he was a man of good standing among the believers, who numbered about 120 at that time (v. 15), as he is one of only two names put forward as possible candidates. The whole community prays for God's guidance and trusts him to show his clear choice. It all sounds fair and reasonable, and yet I wonder how Matthias felt as he took on this role. The others had all been hand-picked by Jesus, whereas he was filling in a gap left by Judas.

I can identify with Matthias. Can you? That sense of being personally called by Jesus – hand-picked for a role – doesn't always happen. Sometimes it's simply a case of having the right skill set to fill a gap or being encouraged by others to step into a new role. It can be daunting, but in God's goodness, we often receive assurance that we are in the right place once we begin the work before us.

Matthias was willing to accept the views of others and to trust in God's guiding hand. May we too be open to God's leading, however he chooses to direct us.

Pray for anyone you know who may lack confidence in their role, that they will know God's assurance and equipping as they go about their tasks.

JACKIE HARRIS

BRF Ministries

Inspiring people of all ages to grow in Christian faith

BRF Ministries is the home of Anna Chaplaincy, Living Faith, Messy Church and Parenting for Faith

As a charity, our work would not be possible without fundraising and gifts in wills.
To find out more and to donate,
visit brf.org.uk/give or call +44 (0)1235 462305

Registered with
FUNDRAISING
REGULATOR

Garden Song brings together original artwork by artist Micah Hayns and reflections and prayers by the Revd Clare Hayns. Leading the reader through 30 selected psalms, the mother–son duo capture the essence of this ancient text – the worship, the grieving and the joy – and open up new ways to engage with its riches. There is also a playlist of suggested music to accompany the reflections.

Garden Song
Exploring the psalms through paintings, reflections and prayers
Clare Hayns and Micah Hayns

978 1 80039 237 3 £14.99
brfonline.org.uk

In this Lenten journey, Jo Swinney explores the broader impact of the Easter story on God's relationship with creation. Through Bible readings, reflections and stories from A Rocha's global conservation efforts, discover how the cross transforms not just our own individual connection with Jesus, but also our relationships with each other and our world.

The Whole Easter Story
Why the cross is good news for all creation
Jo Swinney
978 1 80039 269 4 £9.99
brfonline.org.uk

order

Delivery times within the UK are normally 15 working days. Prices are correct at the time of going to press but may change without prior notice.

le	Price	Qty	Total
y by Day with God (Jan–Apr 2025) – single copy	£4.99		
y by Day with God (May–Aug 2025) – single copy	£5.25		
rden Song	£14.99		
e Whole Easter Story	£9.99		
ding Flourishing	£8.99		

POSTAGE AND PACKING CHARGES			
er value	UK	Europe	Rest of world
er £7.00	£2.00		
0–£29.99	£3.00	Available on request	Available on request
.00 and over	FREE		

Total value of books	
Donation	
Postage and packing	
Total for this order	

ase complete in BLOCK CAPITALS

tle _____ First name/initials _____ Surname _____

ddress _____

_____ Postcode _____

cc. No. _____ Telephone _____

mail _____

ethod of payment

❑ Cheque (made payable to BRF)   ❑ MasterCard / Visa

ard no. ☐☐☐☐ ☐☐☐☐ ☐☐☐☐ ☐☐☐☐

xpires end ☐☐ ☐☐ Security code ☐☐☐   Last 3 digits on the reverse of the card

will use your personal data to process this order.
m time to time we may send you information about
work of BRF Ministries. Please contact us if you wish to discuss
ur mailing preferences. Our privacy possible is available
rf.org.uk/privacy.

ease return this form to:

F Ministries, 15 The Chambers, Vineyard, Abingdon OX14 3FE | **enquiries@brf.org.uk**

r terms and cancellation information, please visit **brfonline.org.uk/terms**.

Each issue of *Day by Day with God* is available from Christian bookshops everywhere. Copies may also be available through your church book agent or from the person who distributes Bible reading notes in your church.

Alternatively, you may obtain *Day by Day with God* on subscription direct from the publisher. There are two kinds of subscription:

Individual subscription
covering 3 issues for 4 copies or less, payable in advance
(including postage & packing).

To order, please complete the details on page 144 and return with the appropriate payment to: BRF Ministries, 15 The Chambers, Vineyard, Abingdon OX14 3FE

You can also use the form on page 144 to order a gift subscription for a friend.

To set up a reoccurring subscription, please go to
brfonline.org.uk/dbdwg-subscription

Group subscription
covering 3 issues for 5 copies or more, sent to one UK address (post free).

Please note that the annual billing period for group subscriptions runs from 1 May to 30 April.

To order, please complete the details on page 143 and return with the appropriate payment to: BRF Ministries, 15 The Chambers, Vineyard, Abingdon OX14 3FE

You will receive an invoice with the first issue of notes.

All our Bible reading notes can be ordered online by visiting
brfonline.org.uk/collections/subscriptions

All subscription enquiries should be directed to:
BRF Ministries, 15 The Chambers, Vineyard, Abingdon OX14 3FE
+44 (0)1865 319700 | **enquiries@brf.org.uk**

To set up a reoccurring subscription, please go to
brfonline.org.uk/dbdwg-subscription

The group subscription rate for *Day by Day with God* will be £15.75 per person until April 2026.

☐ I would like to take out a group subscription for .... (quantity) copies.

☐ Please start my order with the May 2025 / September 2025 / January 2026* issue. I would like to pay annually/receive an invoice* with each edition of the notes. (*delete as appropriate)

Please do not send any money with your order. Send your order to BRF Ministries and we will send you an invoice.

Name and address of the person organising the group subscription:

Title .... First name/initials .... Surname ....

Address...

.... Postcode ....

Telephone .... Email ....

Church...

Name and address of the person paying the invoice if the invoice needs to be sent directly to them:

Title .... First name/initials .... Surname ....

Address...

.... Postcode ....

Telephone .... Email ....

We will use your personal data to process this order. From time to time we may send you information about the work of BRF Ministries. Please contact us if you wish to discuss your mailing preferences. Our privacy policy is available at **brf.org.uk/privacy.**

Please return this form to:
BRF Ministries, 15 The Chambers, Vineyard, Abingdon OX14 3FE
enquiries@brf.org.uk

For terms and cancellation information, please visit **brfonline.org.uk/terms**.

DAY BY DAY WITH GOD INDIVIDUAL/GIFT SUBSCRIPTION FORM

> To order online, please visit **brfonline.org.uk/collections/subscriptions**

☐ I would like to give a gift subscription (please provide both names and addresses)

☐ I would like to take out a subscription myself (complete your name and address details only once)

Title .... First name/initials .... Surname ....

Address ....

.... Postcode ....

Telephone .... Email ....

Gift subscription name ....

Gift subscription address ....

.... Postcode ....

Gift subscription (20 words max. or include your own gift card):

....

....

Please send *Day by Day with God* beginning with the May 2025 / September 2025 / January 2026 issue (*delete as appropriate*):

(*please tick box*)	**UK**	**Europe**	**Rest of world**
1-year subscription	☐ £21.30	☐ £29.55	☐ £35.25
2-year subscription	☐ £40.20	N/A	N/A

Optional donation to support the work of BRF Ministries £ ....

Total enclosed £ .... (cheques should be made payable to 'BRF')

Please charge my MasterCard / Visa with £ ....

Card no. ☐☐☐☐ ☐☐☐☐ ☐☐☐☐ ☐☐☐☐

Expires end [M][M] [Y][Y] Security code ☐☐☐ Last 3 digits on the reverse of the card

We will use your personal data to process this order. From time to time we may send you information about the work of BRF Ministries. Please contact us if you wish to discuss your mailing preferences. Our privacy policy is available at **brf.org.uk/privacy.**

Please return this form to:

BRF Ministries, 15 The Chambers, Vineyard, Abingdon OX14 3FE
enquiries@brf.org.uk

For terms and cancellation information, please visit **brfonline.org.uk/terms.**

Bible Reading Fellowship is a charity (233280) and company limited by guarantee (301324), registered in England and Wales

DBDWG0125